D1452419

The
Enneagram Journey
To New Life

Robert J. Nogosek, C.S.C.

Dimension Books, Inc.
Denville, New Jersey 07834

DEDICATED

to

Patrick H. O'Leary

and

Maria Beesing, O.P.

good friends and pioneers

in the application of the enneagram

to contemporary spirituality

ISBN 0-87193-287-3

Robert J. Nogosek, C.S.C., as author of this book, has made use of material in the book *THE ENNEAGRAM: A Journey of Self Discovery,* which he co-authored by Maria Beesing, O.P. and Patrick H. O'Leary, S.J., and which was published by Dimension Books, Inc., in 1984. Through the use of the theories in that co-authored book in seminars and workshops, Robert J. Nogosek has developed additional ideas to integrate the enneagram with contemporary spirituality. These theories and ideas are different and distinct from those expounded by Mr. Ichazo. Neither Robert J. Nogosek, nor Dimension Books, Inc., is affiliated with Arica Institute, Inc., nor has this book been endorsed or authorized by Arica Institute, Inc., or by Mr. Ichazo. Arica Institute Press is the publisher of numerous books and other publications written by Oscar Ichazo that describe Mr. Ichazo's theories of the "enneagons." *For further information concerning the theory of the enneagons, please contact:* **Arica Institute, Inc., 150 Fifth Avenue, New York, NY 10011. Tel. 212-807-9600.**

TABLE OF CONTENTS

FOREWORD

This book is a result of workshops on the enneagram that I have been giving annually for the past three years to novices of my Holy Cross community at Cascade, Colorado. I have continued to use as my basic source the book on the enneagram I co-authored more than ten years ago, entitled *The Enneagram: A Journey of Self Discovery.*[1] More and more I see the importance of teaching the SPIRITUALITY of the enneagram which that book sought to popularize. Once people have discovered their enneagram number they need to be challenged to take the road to "recovery," to moderate and even completely overcome the way they are addicted to self-fantasy by a specific type of pride. Already it is something of a liberation to accept that we are a certain number with a describable compulsion, since we now can make a choice whether or not to follow our instinctive patterns. However, in order to be truly liberated from our compulsion, we need a thoroughgoing change in the instincts of our personality, in the idea we have of ourselves, and in our affective dispositions. Too often I see work on the enneagram neglecting or simply overlooking the direction to be taken for self-realization as prescribed by the enneagram system. For this reason, in this new book I will go back over much of the material known as the "Jesuit tradition," and re-work its material dealing with *personal conversion* for greater clarity.

Since my recent workshops have been based on the book mentioned above,—which I find so much a part of myself,—this new work follows closely its terminology. I

---

[1] Maria Beesing, O.P., Robert J. Nogosek, C.S.C., Patrick H. O'Leary, S.J., Dimension Books, Inc., Denville, New Jersey, 1984.

think the reader will benefit from the growth in my own understanding of the distinct personalities and their specific spiritualities. As a teacher I have made considerable efforts to unify the material so that the reader does not have to page backward and forward to derive a comprehensive understanding of his or her own type. To simplify the use of inclusive language I have used the first person singular in the presentations. At the same time this use of the first person singular expresses my growing identification with each of the types from the practice I have had in using this enneagram system for over ten years, and from recognizing the enneagram type of most of my close friends and associates. In some way, too, as a Christian humanist I feel that I participate in each of the personality types, while all the while being firmly rooted in my own "Fiveness."

I wish to acknowledge certain persons who have made this book possible. First of all, there are the two who introduced me to the Jesuit tradition of the enneagram: Patrick H. O'Leary, and Maria Beesing, O.P. They have dedicated far more time than I to comprehending and transmitting to others the enneagram system, and were it not for them I would have hardly anything to say in the matter. It was their workshops I followed in the early 1980's which made it possible for me to collaborate with them in the book which we published together in 1984. It became a best-seller in English, and had foreign editions published in Japanese, German, Spanish, French, and Italian. Before I met them through their workshops, they had already been collaborating for seven years in the study and presentation of the enneagram. Even before that, Maria Beesing has been giving enneagram workshops and Patrick O'Leary had participated in the collaborative study of the enneagram by Jesuits at Loyola University in Chicago in 1971-2. Whatever history of the enneagram I know comes basically from Maria and Patrick. In addition I am grateful to Maria for taking the time and trouble to look over this manuscript and make helpful suggestions to me for corrections and additions.

I wish to give additional acknowledgment of my gratitude to Suzanne Brown and Jeanette Arnquist, for their encouragement and helpful comments as readers of the numerous drafts of the manuscript, to Dr. Felicia Czerwionka-Hartnett, for working many hours on the final redaction of the manuscript, and again to Suzanne Brown, for the art work, including the cover design. I also wish to thank my provincial, Rev. Carl F. Ebey, C.S.C., and the Indiana Province of Holy Cross, for granting me a sabbatical leave from my pastorate, enabling me to complete this work.

INTRODUCTION

In following the general pattern of my recent workshops on the enneagram as spirituality, I have divided this work into three sections. SECTION A devotes a chapter to the portrait of each of the nine enneagram personality types, grouping together its characteristics according to the following plan:

How Am I as a .....?

My Gifts

My Childhood

My Pride

Time

Talking Style

Avoidance

Attributes from Ego-Fixation *(several items)*

Fulfillment

Preferred Center

Where Do I Want To Go as a .....?

Not Moving with the Arrow

Moving Against the Arrow *(Instinctual Conversion)*

From Traps to Holy Ideas *(Intellectual Conversion)*

From Passion to Virtue *(Affective Conversion)*

Totems

SECTION B begins with a chapter sketching several ways in which the enneagram system has similarities with the Jungian personality types, especially as discovered through the famous Myers-Briggs Type Indicator. In my workshops invariably questions are asked about the correspondence of the enneagram with the Myers-Briggs Type Indicator, since participants are usually already familiar with the latter and knew their Jungian type. My discussion in this chapter is fairly brief and has as its purpose solely to help the reader move from the possibly better-known Jungian characterology to the lesser-known enneagram system. For readers not already familiar with Carl Jung's system, it may be better simply to skip this initial chapter of Section B.

CHAPTER 11 treats the differentiation of the nine enneagram types. It highlights the concept of fulfillment as explaining why we choose a certain way to be a person, which results in compulsive behavior. The quest for fulfillment is a healthy, God-given impulse, but it is distorted when we see our fulfillment as "self-fulfillment," i.e., as something we can attain solely through our own efforts and strategies. In my opinion, much teaching on the enneagram today does not lead people to transcend the quest for autonomous self-fulfillment. This could be because the secular, scientific culture in the United States bypasses the experience of God's action in our lives. I would argue that as long as we think we can reach personal fulfillment by ourselves, we will continually fall back into what caused our compulsion in the first place when we suffered what the enneagram calls "the fall from society."

CHAPTER 12 concerns the three enneagram centers, or functions, and also my own theory on "wings." In my usage, wings partake in the characteristics of an adjacent *center*, rather than of an adjacent *type*, because I find this more insightful and more true. If the reader has already heard people talking about their "wing," they probably were referring to an adjacent type rather than to an adjacent center. Nonetheless, my presentation in this book of wings as pertaining to an adjacent center is consistent with the material on wings in *The Enneagram: A Journey of Self Discovery.*

The final three chapters deal in depth with overcoming our compulsion by a three-fold conversion: instinctive, intellectual, and affective. These chapters pick up again what was briefly stated in Section A on "Where Do I Want to Go as a ....?" By logic, the intellectual conversion should precede the other two types of conversion, since how we see reality is basic to our holistic conversion; however, it is easier for the reader to grasp and use these insights on conversion in the order in which I present them. In simple terms, our conscious life is made up of thoughts, feelings and external behavior. We cannot by will power make ourselves feel in a certain way, but we can alter our feelings by changing our pattern of thinking and/or by changing our way of behaving. It seems easier simply to begin our quest to change our personality by altering our external behavior, and only after that try to change our way of thinking. For this reason I begin with instinctive conversion and then move to intellectual conversion, before concluding with affective conversion.

SECTION C provides the reader with a *glossary* of enneagram terms. The enneagram system does have its own specific terminology, and even I myself at times wonder how to explain clearly such terms as "traps" and the "prides." These definitions of enneagram terms can sharpen our understanding and keep our minds on track about the enneagram system, at least according to the Jesuit tradition. Perhaps in subsequent editions of this book this glossary will grow through my own continued experience in using the enneagram and through contributions from others.

It is only in the past few years that I have been giving workshops on the enneagram. Before that, my practice was to give enneagram retreats, where participants had six to eight days of prayerful meditations based on the gospels.

That material was published in a book entitled *The Nine Portraits of Jesus.*[1] I hope this present book is seen as carrying on that retreat spirit. I have included many scripture references, not to prove that St. Paul, for example, can be seen as knowing the enneagram, but as a way of showing that being freed from compulsion is very much a concern in New Testament writings. This book that you are about to begin to study contains the attitude that the work of the Spirit in our personality neither rides above our natural dispositions and instincts, nor outlaws and condemns them, but rather works within our souls like yeast in dough to transform the very wellsprings of our life. As a foundation for this work of the Spirit in us we desperately need to turn over our lives by an "abandonment to God," such as I try to describe in this book. In my opinion, to leave God out of the enneagram system is to forsake a stance of life essential for attaining true personal fulfillment.

> Robert J. Nogosek, C.S.C.
> Our Lady of Soledad Parish
> Coachella, California

---

[1] Robert J. Nogosek, C.S.C., Dimension Books, Inc., Denville, New Jersey, 1987.

A.
Enneagram
Typology

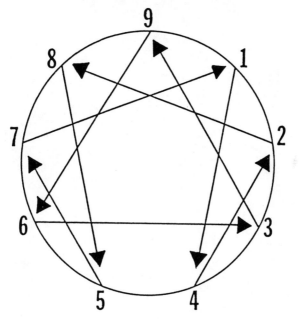

1. THE EXACTING ONE[1]

Where Am I as a One?

My Gifts

As a One, I am dedicated to *perfection*: to being perfect and doing things in a perfect way. This includes a great attention to detail. Because I insist on taking all details seriously, I can point out how quite ordinary events are worth remembering and talking about.

I take pride in being a hard worker. I am always ready to spend extra time on a task, because it is important to me that it be done well. My concern for orderliness and neatness will make any place more attractive and more fitting for human habitation. I really enjoy working hard in an organized way.

I take pride in being direct and honest before others, and I believe in treating everyone fairly and equally. I am an exacting person: I am hard on myself and tend to be hard on others.

My Childhood

As a One I grew up with the idea that unless I am perfect I am not acceptable. This was true for my school work, and for just about everything else. It was expected that I be good, and virtue was a reward in itself. I would hear about it when I made a mistake or did something that was wrong. As a result I became obsessively concerned to do what is right and to avoid what is wrong. Perhaps I had

---

[1] Cf Beesing, et al, pp. 11, 14-19, 51-56, 102, 113, 114-116, 120, 132f, 137, 149, 162f, 171f, 181f, 193-195, 205, 210.

to take on adult responsibilities prematurely. If so, I took this for granted, and did not think I was anyone special in the family just because of the sacrifices I made for others.

My Pride

As a One I feel most alive when making a effort to counteract evil, disorder and error. I interrupt and interfere with reality in order to correct it. I am attracted to activities that promise self-improvement. My greatest pride is in how hard I try to do good and be good. As a hard-working person, I am always ready to put in a great effort to do things well, especially by giving attention to details.

Time

As a One, my attention to detail includes the scheduling of time. I schedule my life in such a way that I effectively eliminate free time. I am often bothered by not getting things done the way they should be done simply because there is not enough time. I tend to want to go over whatever I do so that I do it better.

Talking Style

I give myself away as a One by doing a lot of pointing when I talk. I also like to make a point. In writing I do a lot of underlining to get my point across. I can be very talkative and even bubbly. People may notice in my voice a certain irritability of which I am not usually conscious.

Avoidance

I need to learn that what I avoid as a One is *anger*. This means I have inside myself a lot of unacknowledged resentment. For me to be good is to be perfect, and I see anger as an imperfection I should not have. There is plenty of reason for me to be angry because I think everything should be perfect: myself, others, and the world around me. Since that good of perfection often is not attained, the result within me is anger because the good I love is being blocked. Such *dissatisfaction* causes me to be on edge. The repression of my anger provokes an unspoken intolerance for the ways things are. I am generally dissatisfied about something.

As a One, I tend to be preoccupied with faults: my own, first of all, and then those of others. In my thoughts I keep adding to the collection of faults. This bothers me a lot. I try hard to improve myself by going back over the past, and checking out what I did wrong.

Besides avoiding the recognition and expression of my anger, I also tend to suppress inner wishes of my nature. As I see it, I must attend to the *shoulds* in my life. Only after I have done what I *should do* can I let myself consider what things I would *like to do* as enjoyment. To me pleasures should be postponed until everything else gets done. Life is hard, and I think we have to earn our time off.

Resentment

What I need to face about myself as a One is my *resentment*. This is my ego-fixation, the compulsion of my personality type. I get preoccupied with the fact that things never seem to be according to my satisfaction. Because I am a perfectionist, I think it is not right to have things imperfect or untidy.

Meticulousness

As a One I am a real stickler for details. How a thing is done is very important to me. Neatness is very important, along with cleanliness. I like to review the past, especially the day I have just lived. I don't want to miss anything that needs to be checked out. I tend to be slow in making decisions because all the details have to be studied beforehand. If I am the boss, I tend to delay risky decisions, and to fill my time with complicated procedures.

The Inner Critic

A salient characteristic of being a One is my *inner critic.* It is hard for me to believe that other personalities lack this internal monitor of their conduct. It is like an inner voice which continually checks up on me. It keeps telling me to go back over past behavior to see where I might have been wrong in what I did. My inner critic never lets me put to rest any issue of right or wrong. Even what I am thinking is judged. I know that my penchant for self-criticism also gets projected as criticism of others. I really am a critical person.

A Divided House[2]

It seems like the inner critic lives in the main part of my house, and then I have a cellar in my being where anything might be going on. Sometimes I even feel that instead of being a divided house, I am really a dormant volcano, and that I could blow any time if I let go of my hid-

---

[2] I am indebted to Helen Palmer for this metaphor of a divided house as describing the One. Cf Helen Palmer, *THE ENNEAGRAM. Understanding Yourself and the Others in Your Life,* Harper, San Francisco, 1988, p. 76.

den inner feelings. I insist that all the feelings, memories, and desires that are hidden away underneath are to give an account of themselves to my inner critic; otherwise I will not feel good about myself. I feel resentful when I see others following their own base desires instead of doing what they know they should do to avoid bad conduct. I don't see how people can just do whatever they feel like doing and still feel good about themselves.

Fulfillment

My inner critic tends to be my guide to self-fulfillment, as though it had a wisdom and authority superior to my own thinking. Only by correcting what is wrong and doing what is right do I see life as being led as it should be. Since there is so much to correct, I put my main energy into trying to make better the situation outside me. To me, there is one correct solution for every situation. I am apt to be insistent that others accept the correctness to which I have dedicated myself. I experience myself as smaller than the world, and so I have to work hard to get on top of things. To reach fulfillment in life, I seem always to be working uphill.

Preferred Center

As a One I have chosen my gut center as my preferred center for functioning as a person. I feel at home just being present in a situation and trusting in my spontaneous reactions. I have a wing on my heart center, and as such I do have a deep concern for the feelings and needs of others. I try to get others to respond to me in a positive way. My blind spot is in my neglected head center. I tend to substitute my instinctive function for thinking, and get myself bogged down in some small detail, instead of trying

7

to see objectively how everything fits together, and how I fit in. If I am managing other persons, I tend to intervene too much into what should be the responsibility of another person, instead of putting my main effort into providing a vision for others. At times others suffer from the bias in my thinking, and the way I stubbornly impose my animus on them.

Where Do I Want To Go as a One?

Not Moving With the Arrow

I need to work uphill against my own compulsion of resentment, and not let myself get sucked down by moving with the arrow of compulsion. For me that movement toward greater compulsion would take on the added compulsion of the ego-melancholy *Four*. As a One I am generally an optimistic person; for me to lose that hope for improvement would result in depression, making me moody. This can happen if I become overwhelmed by a mountain of work, and have neither the time nor the energy to do any of my tasks really well, so that I end up not trying at all. For me to stop trying to be perfect is to throw in the towel and become a basket case.

Moving Against the Arrow

Instead of losing myself in greater compulsiveness, I need to act against my compulsion of resentment by moving against the arrow toward the pride of the *Seven*. Sevens are fun-loving; they want to enjoy life. As a One I need to have greater confidence in the wisdom and good sense of what is down deep in the cellar of my house. To give my attention to the cellar means that I must pay much less attention to my inner critic upstairs. I should recognize once and for all that the inner critic is not the voice of my conscience, but instead comes from how I grew up. I have simply internalized the critical voice of others, especially my parents. In order to become whole as a person, I need to befriend my desires and feelings, instead of subjecting them to suspicion and criticism.

Moving against the arrow of compulsion to become more like a Seven is not going to feel right for me, but I need to trust that taking on the pride of the Seven will give me much more balance. Being so exacting has made me less than human, and has cut me off from living harmoniously with others. I have tended to set myself up as superior to others, as though I am much more ethical and righteous than they are. Discovering that my inner critic actually stems from an inner compulsion can help free me from its voice. I know I need also to listen to other parts of my being, and accept all that I am. I also need to listen to others,—friends, especially,—who want me to become less serious and who see in me an ability to have fun and be silly. Hopefully, they know how to tease me, even though I don't know how to tease them back with the same playfulness.

Even though some Ones end up living a double life,—one very strict and hard working, and the other loose and licentious,—I do want to live just one life. I don't want a divided house. Even though it does not feel right, I need to imitate the spontaneity of persons who are Sevens, and appreciate the way a Seven is an "eternal child." Most likely as a One I missed out on a lot of play as a child, but I have within myself a real desire to have fun, to chat a lot, to tell funny stories, and to go to silly parties. By the way I repress my deep passions, I am trying to be something I am not. Such *prudishness* can make me appear very funny to

9

others, and set me up for teasing. I know I always will be a One, but more and more I intend to appreciate how good it is for me to be more teasable and playful, instead of always wanting to correct what is wrong or imperfect.

From Traps to Holy Ideas

My trap as a One is my idea of *perfection*. For me "to be is to be perfect." I think things have to be perfect right now, and that the slightest imperfection spoils everything. Consequently I tend to find fault constantly with myself, with others, and with my environment, just because some perfection is missing. As I keep trying harder to make things perfect, I become impatient, and others find it hard to live with my fussiness and irritability.

Intellectual conversion for me as a One means to shed this obsession with perfection, and to accept the gradual and evolutionary way in which creation is ruled by God. God works to better creation through drawing out the good in gradual steps of growth. This holy idea of GROWTH needs to replace my trap of perfection. It means that to be good is to be in the process of becoming more. Holiness itself is a journey rather than the attainment of some norm of being complete and correct.

One of the great Christian paradoxes states that to be perfect we must accept our imperfection. Mistakes themselves can lead to goodness, for God is able to draw good out of evil. Like God, I am to be tolerant and patient with what is evil or imperfect, lest I trample out the good which may be there only in seed form. What looks like a terrible messiness can actually have a glorious outcome.

I want to accept being a creature called to a process of growth, to be a human being "on the way." Rather than rejecting the whole because some part is missing or out of place, I want to believe in the good that I see, and in its power to become more. As St. Paul states, we should fill our minds "with those things that are good and that deserve praise: things that are true, noble, right, pure, lovely, and honorable."[3]

From Passion to Virtue

I now see that I have been blind to my *resentment*, to this anger which has been a ruling passion in my life. I took for granted that my fulfillment consisted in making things perfect. As a result there was always something about which to be critical, always something not in right order or not done correctly. My reaction was anger. Through this anger I was saying to others that it is more important that things be done correctly, than that we get along with one another and live in peace. Often my critical attitude centered on small and even unimportant details, and this made it difficult for others to feel at home with me because of my being such a perfectionist.

By letting go of the trap of perfection and accepting the holy idea of growth, I can allow myself to be a creature among others under God's rule. This will lead me into greater peace and *serenity*. Such serenity is a healing for my passion of *anger*. I will no longer want to be so exacting as a person. Instead of looking at what is wrong, I want now to focus my attention on accepting the good that is there, limited as it may be, and to believe in the process of growth.

In such serenity of heart I will be able to see a wonderful complementarity in all of creation as a sacred

---

[3] Ph 4:8

11

dance of opposites. I myself am made up of contrasts and opposite poles which can come together in wholeness and balance, once I am much more tolerant and patient with myself. Rather than be a house divided, I will be able to see the wonder of all my parts, and trust there is no explosive force within me to lead me astray. Instead of assuming that my inner critic is a voice of righteousness, I can now recognize that there are many voices in myself. I am to accept all that is within me as together constituting who I am as a person.

Totems

As a compulsed One I tended to be like a *terrier*, always worrying about what was going on around me and "snapping at heels" by pointing out to others what is not being done right.

In working to be freed of my compulsion I see myself more as an ANT, putting my whole being into the organized work I do with others. Rather than shoving and pushing others, I want to cooperate with them for our common ideals. Just as an ant can move great loads, I feel fulfilled in getting a great deal done in the tasks I do with others. I also appreciate better my need and ability to communicate intimately with others at close range, similar to the way ants communicate with their antennae.

2. THE INGRATIATING TWO[1]

Where Am I as a Two?

My Gifts

As a Two, I am dedicated to being helpful. I am ready to make great sacrifices to help another. I am always ready to welcome another into my home. I am kind, sensitive and concerned about what is good for others.

I put a high value on personal relationships. I welcome others with outstretched arms. I want to touch others, to take them by the hand and make them feel comfortable and happy. I want others to feel important and loved. For this reason I can draw out the best from others.

I am a non-judgmental person. When others make mistakes I don't condemn them, but try to help them in the bad consequences of their mistakes. By nature I am compassionate.

My Childhood

As a child I was probably daddy's little girl, or mommy's little man. I came to know the qualities I had that were appealing to different adults, and I could put on a performance to make each person like me. In this way I developed the ability to sense the inner wishes of others, and adapt myself to them in order to win their affection.

---

[1] Cf Beesing, et al, pp. 11, 19-23, 57-62, 103, 110f, 116, 120, 128f, 138, 150, 163f, 172, 182f, 195f, 206, 213.

My Pride

As a Two I am proud of being helpful, especially to any person who is special to me. I feel important when another is dependent on my help. I see the world full of needy people, and I seek out people who need my help.

Time

I value time mainly in terms of being used for personal relationships. For me a good time is interpersonal, and what is impersonal is a bad time. Time drags when I cannot enter well into a relationship, but time is well spent when I can get closer to another. I generally do not like meetings. My time at a meeting is worthwhile only to the extent I can experience personal encounter. As a Two, I tend to live in the time of another whose attention I have won by my care and concern.

Talking Style

My interests are generally limited to persons who are special to me. I talk about the needs of people I know and love, rather than about the world's problems. I avoid abstract thinking except to the extent that it could be useful to someone I know. I am very sincere in my admiration of others, and I tend to overlook those mistakes of others which got them into trouble.

Avoidance

As a Two I avoid recognizing that I have *needs*. I focus on the needs of others, especially the needs which I can meet. Because I do not like to admit I need others for any help, I often have a hard time knowing what I want for myself other than sharing the lives of those who need me. I dislike self-analysis. I feel it is wrong to focus attention on myself, and as regards others, I want to help them rather than analyze them.

Flattery

As a Two, what I need to recognize about myself is my propensity to *flattery*. I present myself in such a way to another in order to gratify that person, and so win approval and affection. This is really a form of *seduction* which I fail to recognize in myself. Actually I have a deep need for appreciation from others, and I seek to obtain this appreciation by catering to a need or wish I have discovered in another. Over the years I have developed a great sensitivity to the moods and preferences of others, so as to be able to cater to what pleases them. In this way I am able to win their affection, and create a personal relationship with them. I do not feel good about myself unless I have gained such attention, appreciation and approval from another.

Multiple Selves

Because I change myself to suit the needs of those who are important to me, I may experience myself as multiple selves. To ensure my own popularity, I choose to become the personality that will please the special other, but in the long run I wonder who is the real me. At times it seems that different parts of me are parceled out to different friends, but nobody knows my whole person, not even myself. Because of this parceling out of myself differently to different people, I have a fear of intimacy, for if anyone got really close to me, they might see that I am really not the person they thought I was, but that I just adapted myself to please them.

Independence

As a Two, I consider myself superior to others because I see myself as very *selfless*, always thinking of the needs of others and never of my own needs. Some other people, however, will experience me as a very independent person, because I will not let them serve any need in myself. Since I am always controlling the relationship by trying to put the other in a situation of need for me, the other finds it difficult to relate with me.

Fulfillment

As a Two I need to be needed. To me fulfillment consists in forming the kind of personal relationships in which I preserve my independence while making the other dependent on me. I take the initiative in forming such relationships by moving toward others to make them feel cared about and cared for. I do not feel good as a person unless I experience the approval and appreciation of those whose needs and desires I have served. I feel proud of myself when I help others without their helping me in return.

Preferred Center

I have chosen my way to be a person mainly through the function of my heart center. I am habitually concerned about personal relationships. I want people to like me a lot. I feel appreciated and loved through making others feel important. I am always concerned with what will help others feel loved.

As a Two I have a wing on my gut center. I do want to be the center of attention in any group and I feel more myself when I am reacting spontaneously to another. What I neglect is the function of my head center. I habitually talk about relationships and persons special to me rather than about politics or world affairs. I feel a meeting is of value only if I can do something for another. It do not care to spend time with others planning or considering how we can make an institution operate better. Abstract thinking is boring to me, it seems irrelevant to what is important.

Where Do I Want To Go as a Two?

Not Moving With the Arrow

If a significant other in my life does not respond to my care with appreciation I am likely to feel highly offended. Such hurt can cause me to want to take revenge. With feelings of aggression I may strike out against that person, especially by bitter and belittling words. Such angry feelings could then lead me to a depression in which I feel I can no longer respond to anybody's needs because no one, not even God, appreciates me.

What has happened is that I have moved with the arrow of compulsion toward the ego-vengeance *Eight*. This can very easily occur because my sense of fulfillment is so dependent on how another reacts to me. This is very unhealthy, for I am compounding my compulsion of co-dependency as a Two with the aggressiveness characteristic of the Eight.

Moving Against the Arrow

Instead of compounding my compulsion of trying to please by moving with the arrow, I will want to act against my compulsion by moving against the arrow toward the pride of the *Four*, who says, "I am unique." Fours see their value in the special feelings they have through their experiences of joy and sorrow. To have the pride of the Four can free me from the craving to win approval through adapting myself to please others. Instead of trying to please by helping another I concentrate on being appreciated for my own life story and my own deep feelings. I come to see I am a special person because of my sensitive feelings and all the sufferings I have endured. I begin to give attention to the authentic expression of my deepest feelings, so that another may know me and thereby love me as a very special person. Although initially to take on the pride of the Four may seem wrong and make me feel very insecure, the enneagram tells me that this is the route to take to get in better touch with myself and to begin to relate to others in a more satisfying way. To do this, however, I need to discover what love really is.

From Traps to Holy Ideas

My problem is that I have been trapped by a false idea of love, namely, that love is simply *service*. Because of this idea of serving others, I think of myself as totally self-less, whereas in reality I am very dependent on appreciation from those I serve. My help typically has strings attached and I will reproach those who do not give love in return. All this concern to help others has the false foundation of fulfilling my own need for appreciation. This trap of service leads to possessiveness and manipulation of those I believe I am loving.

Only when I become dissatisfied with myself as a co-dependent person can I become open to the holy idea of GRACE. Most likely all along I have been relating to God as I have related to others, namely, by seeking to gratify God by doing something to please. It is really a strategy of winning God's love and appreciation of me. By it, however, I actually miss the message of grace. That message is that there is no way to win God's love; it is always a *gift*. The very meaning of grace is divine gift, and that divine gift is unconditional love. God invites me to a relationship built on that gift of grace, rather than on anything I do for God. I am made *worthy* by God's love for me. God does not love me because I am good; I am good because God loves me.

It is all a matter of understanding what love is. If love is won or earned or purchased,[2] then it is no longer love. That is true in my relationship with God. It is also true in my relationship with other persons. As a Two I need to learn this idea, breathe in this idea, and shout out this idea from the housetops: *I believe in the gift of love*, in the gift of another's love for me. I believe in grace.

There just is no way of relating properly to God without allowing that I am loved by God for who I am rather than for what I have done for God. This is why Jesus stressed the Fatherhood of God: a parent's love is like this. A parent loves the child before the child loves the parent, and a good parent instinctively always loves the child because of who the child is, one's own son or daughter. We need this parental idea of God, rather than the idea of an authoritarian Master, who, like Santa Claus, gives gifts to those who are good, and not to those who are bad.

Once accepted, the holy idea of grace can have tremendous consequences for me as a Two. Once I find out that God loves me *unconditionally,* I can change my idea of what love is in personal relationships. Since God loves me however I am, I may be able to see that this is also how others may love me. My personality as a Two has been formed

---

[2] Cf Song of Songs 8:7.

19

with doing what I can to get love. Now I see I can be appreciated because of how I am, not because of what I have done. To reveal my true self,—*how* I really am,—can open the way to receiving love. Since I now *believe in love* I can dare say: "To know me is to love me." Now I want to know myself, I want to discover and articulate the feelings that are me so that another can know me, and thus be moved to love me truly for who I am. This is to discover Love as gift, mutual gift between persons. I see that to show my love is not so much to do something for another as to show myself and share myself as a gift to another.

In this way I discover the *mystery* of love as a reality I can know only by getting involved with another. Up to now, as a Two, I have been treating love like a problem, like something I could attain by my own efforts of pleasing others and catering to their needs. I was actually controlling my relationships. To get into love as a *mystery*, however, I must lose control. I cannot make another love me. It is that person's decision and free gift. To be the beloved of another thus leads me to awe and the surrender that lets the other know me as I am. The only proper reaction to another's gift of self to me is to disclose myself.

Such surrender elicits from me a new appreciation of life, and can lead me to contemplation. As long as I tried to relate to God by doing something for God I found both mental prayer and prayer of quiet burdensome and unattractive, because by such prayer I was not doing anything for God, nor was I really doing much of anything.. Discovering the mystery of love calms and quiets me. So much around me is revealing its truth and beauty! I want to be one with the All!

From Passion to Virtue

Having uncovered the false idea, or *trap*, of service and surrendered myself to the holy idea of grace, I now am ready to deal directly with my passion of *pride*. It really did not occur to me as a Two that my predominant vice was pride. I didn't think of myself as actually having a predominant fault. I had been thinking of myself as good because of all I did for others. Now I see I was gratifying others, that they think of me and need me. I was serving others to get something from them for myself, that they would appreciate having me in their life. To feel worthwhile I had somehow to be an appendage to another, and so I had to win from that other a need for me. That really was not love, nor was it selflessness. It was catering and manipulating.

Another reason I thought I was especially good was because I disregarded my own needs. I saw myself as serving others, but I did not see them as serving me. I evaluated this as being *selfless*, but I was actually exercising a subtle control over them by making them need me and by not letting them serve me. How real were my affections for them? Was I not really trying to make myself the center of attention and affection? If so, wasn't that really pride?

Others sensed my pride in myself by the surprising *independence* that was characteristic of me. After all, being proud is saying, "I do not need you." Wasn't I saying precisely that by denying I had needs? Once I discovered the holy idea of grace my eyes were opened. I saw as never before that being loved is *humbling*. Letting myself be loved is not controlling at all. I am at the mercy of the other person deciding to love me and cherishing me as I am, warts and all. In fact, not to be loved that way is not to be loved at all.

21

Humility is to say, "I have need of you," and to let myself be known as I really am. This is how I am, a needy person ready to let myself be known and held in another's heart. It is letting oneself be known for however one is, trusting that the other will accept gratefully the open gift I make of myself. Humility is respecting the freedom of others and not making them owe me their love. When I am loved I am in awe that another should cherish me,—because it is so *undeserved*! I have not earned their love. They just decided to love me. What a wonder!

Totems

As a compulsed Two I was like a *cat*. I was affectionate, but carried an air of independence by not letting others do for me. I liked to get close to people, but controlled how close they could get to me. In working to be freed of my compulsion, I see myself more as an IRISH SETTER. I can now give the warmth of love with no strings attached. I respect the freedom of others. I am open to whatever love another may choose to give me, and I will respond to that love warmly and with gratitude, because it is not something owed to me, but a great gift.

3. THE AMBITIOUS THREE[1]

Where Am I as a Three?

My Gifts

As a Three, I measure my life by my achievements. I put my total commitment into the tasks I undertake, and feel most alive when in the midst of activity. I move directly from ideas into action.

I am also very adaptable: I can quickly move from one project to another. I enjoy working under pressure, and readily give my attention to a number of projects at the same time. This makes me feel I am on top of things.

Since I totally believe in the success of whatever project I undertake, I readily draw others to collaborate with optimism and determination. What we achieve together gives all of us a deep satisfaction in having done something really worthwhile. In this way I can get many people involved in the task and motivated to do a good job.

As I see it, a job should be done in the most efficient way possible. I will insist that in working on a task we have clearly-defined goals and standards for evaluating our performance. This means getting organized and cutting through unnecessary red tape.

As a counselor I am very objective. I believe that in order to have self-esteem a person has to achieve something. I am good at challenging others to put focus into their lives, and to set to work to realize the hopes they have.

---

[1] Cf Beesing, et. al., pp. 11, 23-27, 62-67, 106, 111f, 116f, 120f, 130f, 136f, 150f, 161f, 172f, 184f, 196, 206, 213f.

I inspire and support them in their action, so that by their successes they will come to believe in themselves.

My Childhood

It is likely that as a child I felt loved and esteemed mainly for what I accomplished, especially in competition with others. I worked hard for recognition from others. It was real important to me always to be a winner in whatever I did.

My Pride

As a Three, I am proud of my achievements. I take pride in my innate ability to persuade others to share my goals or to buy what I am selling. I often view myself as superior to others because I am so resourceful and efficient. I feel good about myself only when I am successful in the eyes of others. For me *to be is to be successful.*

Time

I value time as a vehicle for getting something done. Every minute must be used; otherwise it represents a lost opportunity. I see time as very limited, and it cannot be expanded or stretched. Things have to be done on time; after the deadline is too late. I adjust my goals in accordance with how much time is available.

Because I am an *achiever* I tend to take on too much for the time available. As a result I generally run a little late. Although it is nice to start on time and end on time, what is more important to me is simply to get the job done. Time is well spent when something is accomplished. I like to use my time in getting things done. It puzzles me when people need to have a lot of time just for themselves.

I tend not to have much free time, because I keep my schedule packed with activity all day, and even bring some of my work home with me. I am used to doing a number of different things at the same time, or closely scheduled one after the other. To me it really feels good to be that busy. I even like having a "working vacation." I don't really care to have a lot of free time.

Talking Style

As a Three I am a great talker. I don't ever run out of words. I like to get the attention of others and to have an attractive appearance.

Whenever I try to sell something I use my whole personality to convince others to buy it. Some people say I am a "con-artist" because I know how to use words to my own advantage. I know I need to watch myself to avoid trying to persuade others by just putting on a good front. Because I so much want to get ahead and be a success, I notice the tendency in myself to try to deceive others by a feigned sincerity.

Avoidance

As a Three, I identify myself with my achievements. Consequently, I will seek to avoid failure of any sort, even at great cost to myself and others. Even though later on I may turn to something else, I tend to measure the worth of my whole life by the success in what I am doing now. Since I identify my personal worth with what I achieve, I take care to undertake only what has a very good chance of succeeding.

Craving for Success

To understand myself as a Three, I need to recognize my *craving for success*. No one success satisfies me. My achievements are not cumulative; I have to keep on having more and more. Since I try for too many successes, I tend to substitute quantity for quality. I need to admit also that what I call "success" is really the reaction of others to the image I create. It is a competitive thing. I have to be *seen* as a front runner. I want to be valued and loved because my achievements show I am superior to others. Isn't this some kind of pride?

Putting My Feelings in a Sack

My preoccupation with being a success in the eyes of others has a bad effect on what I do with my feelings: I put them in a sack to be looked at some other time. I do not want my personal feelings to get in the way of my efficiency. I can get so caught up in my projects that I have little private and personal life. I tend to *use* those working for me, saying that anyone is replaceable if he or she cannot get the job done. I make it difficult for others to get really close to me because I identify myself so much with my work.

Fulfillment

My fulfillment as a Three consists in being successful. This means that I am esteemed by others because of what I accomplish. I don't see myself fulfilled by achieving what is worthwhile irrespective of what others think. I thus have a compulsion to measure my value by what impresses others.

I am the kind of person that takes initiative in moving out to others to get a favorable reaction from them. I adjust to what will bring me fame. The inner fear of being of little value is alleviated by getting people's admiration because of what I have achieved. This may be in the money I have made, the possessions I have, my social prestige, a job promotion, or whatever else is seen as success in my society. To protect my worth as a person I keep moving out to attain more successes. For me, to be a good person is to achieve something in life.

Preferred Center

As a Three, I am a heart person. This means that I have chosen my feeling center as my preferred way of functioning. Typically I enter a situation and ask myself if these persons are going to like me or not. I seek control by gaining achievements that will get a favorable impression from others. I keep asking myself if others are responding to me.

Even though the feeling function is my preferred way of functioning, I have a problem with my feelings. My being is divided or torn by the fact that instead of living out of my true feelings, as would be expected in a heart person, I use my feeling function to substitute for thinking and instinctive behavior. In order to get others to like me because they see me as an achiever, I present myself before them with a full head of steam for the business at hand, and often hide or repress others feelings, such as affection or fear.

To repress my personal feelings can cause me to lose touch with myself. By tying all my thoughts and feelings to the success I seek, I have little room in my heart left for what is not directed to my work. I fail to appreciate that knowledge is a good in itself, and what I mainly want to know is what will serve my all-consuming concern for success. In neglecting my own cultural development I may be leaving untapped many of my best talents, such as that of entertaining others or expressing feelings in other creative ways. What will happen to my sense of myself should my work fail, or poor health force me into retirement? Will I then be at a loss to know how to live or what to live for? Is the success of my work the whole meaning of my life?

I need to beware of getting out of touch with ordinary life as others lead it. Because my total attention is focused on my goals, I may not notice what others are experiencing, such as their personal problems and other causes of suffering. I can become quite intolerant of my fellow-workers who do not give their whole heart and soul to the work itself. Since what I care about in my own life is my output, I expect others to be the same.

Have I really faced my attitude regarding emotional intimacy? If I identify my value with my achievements, then I am not going to think there is much value is being known simply for who I am. Do I just have to keep putting up a front with my words, and fear to let others know me simply in a personal way? Perhaps my preoccupation with my work is really a subterfuge to avoid intimacy. By using the relational powers of my feeling center to substitute for my instinctive or gut function I make my body language portray an appearance that will get a favorable reaction to what I am selling or promoting. Meanwhile the personal emotions of my feeling center are suspended in the interest of an effective job performance. Eventually it could happen that all I am is the image I portray.

Where Do I Want To Go as a Three?

Not Moving with the Arrow

This enneagram analysis of myself as a Three can be very destructive to my self-esteem. Seeing the falseness of my behavior in my self-seeking for success, I could end up simply rejecting myself. To stop trying to achieve, however, will only compound my problem. It would amount to following the arrow of compulsion to the ego-indolent Nine. I need to see that my drive to achieve is not evil, but only a distortion. What I need to do is to broaden the way I look at my life and my worth. I may be achieving a lot of good, but the distortion comes when I put my heart on appearances. It is not all that bad to love myself and want my own success, but this needs to be extended also to love of others and of God. Recognizing this as a distortion of my energies can help me put my house in order.

As a Three, any experience of failure is likely to cause me to lose faith in myself. There are many books which seek to prevent such disheartenment by demonstrating that out of failure we learn how to be successful. A salient example is that of Thomas Edison's search for the right filament for the light bulb. From each failure he said he saw what would not work, and thus by the process of elimination was making progress to discovering what would work. Christopher Columbus failed in his life goal to find a new route to the Indies, but he did discover America. Such examples may serve to bolster my self-confidence when I face failure, so that I do not move with the arrow of compulsion toward the ego-indolent Nine and become a couch potato. As a Three it is unhealthy for me to become inactive; I need activity and challenge to have reason for living and hoping.

Moving Against the Arrow

What I need to do as a Three is to move against the arrow of compulsion toward the pride of the Six, who says, "I am loyal." I can decide that what makes me good as a person is not my own success but rather my loyalty to those with whom I work and live. This means to focus my efforts on what is greater than myself, such as being bonded with others on a team and being dedicated to the common good of society. I might keep working at what I am doing, but change my motives from self-interest to altruism. Since this is very honorable it should make me feel good about myself.

By taking pride in being loyal as a member of society, I can see that I have something to contribute for the benefit of the common good, and that this contribution is to be made in cooperation with others in a spirit of interdependence. By identifying my efforts with what will better society, I will come to have a sense of satisfaction in whatever benefits the common good, even though this comes about not from my own efforts but from the work of others. I can learn to rejoice because we are all working together, each doing his or her part to make our society better. There can also be a sense of peace that good is being achieved, even though I myself may not be doing it. Should I have to retire from work, I will still be able to encourage others in the work they do for the betterment of society.

Taking pride in being loyal will also affect the relationships I have with my family and personal friends. To be a friend is to be loyal. There is a whole world of satisfaction to be found in being a friend. Maybe I have seen friends as only instruments to my own success. If so, the decision to work on cultivating friendship will open up my preferred heart function to experience the personal communion of sharing truth and love in a way I failed to appreciate in the past. After all, mutual sharing is the touch-stone of life.

From Traps to Holy Ideas

My trap as a Three was my idea of *efficiency,* which evaluated the goodness of a person in terms of that person being able to achieve something. As a Three, I thought that my efficiency made me better than others. This quest for efficiency was tied in with my ambition and expectations. I agreed with the saying that "time is money." All time is very precious but limited, and I believed I needed to use it to achieve success. According to this way of thinking, the purpose of life itself was to get ahead.

Enneagram theory invites me to an intellectual conversion of replacing the trap of efficiency with the holy idea of GOD'S WILL. I am called to dedicate my life to that holy idea by contributing my talents, my time, my efforts, and my money to what God wants to achieve. God's Will is the building up of the Kingdom of God. For God to reign over the world, our activities must serve God's purposes. By such abandonment to God, I will overcome in myself the separation between religion and life. Whatever I do belongs to God and to God's glory. My failures themselves can be used by God to bring about greater good.

Living for the transformation of the world into God's Kingdom can free me from attachment to my own achievements, so that I can rejoice in the accomplishments of others. God's Kingdom is built up by the activities of those who use their God-given talents according to the opportunities they have in order to build a better world. By working for the Lord instead of for myself, I am assured a rich reward in God's Kingdom. As Vatican II states:

> *For after we have obeyed the Lord,*
> *and in His Spirit nurtured on earth the*
> *values of human dignity, brotherhood*
> *and freedom, and indeed all the good*
> *fruits of our nature and enterprise, we*
> *will find them again, but freed of stain,*
> *burnished and transfigured when Christ*
> *hands his Kingdom over to the Father.*[2]

I can thus see that overcoming the split between religion and life involves the recognition of the entire world as properly God's Kingdom, and my call to contribute with others that God's will may be done "on earth as it is in heaven."

From Passion to Virtue

As long as I took success as my fulfillment in life, I tended to use all means, even those that were underhanded, for my own advancement. As a Three, I also tended to put on a false front of pretense to promote or sell whatever would make me a success. Actually I prided myself in this ability to con others, while all the time I was engaged in the vice of *deceit*. It was a subtle and powerful passion. I was actually "deceived by my own deceit," for I considered my cleverness to be one of my great qualities. What was true and good became secondary to what would bring me success.

Having abandoned myself to God's Will, I now know I deceived myself in thinking that success was a measure of my worth. My notion of success was really *vanity*. I was actually a vain person. That now frightens me because vanity means *being empty*. My emptiness inside was from making my outward personality mask what was

---

[2] *Gaudium et Spes, 39.*

really the truth I knew inside myself. Because I tended to hide from others whatever would hinder my own success, I really made my fulfillment consist in *appearances*. My supreme good was only what people thought of me. This had become my god.

To get over such idolatry, I want to put my heart on *truthfulness*. I want to be transparent to others. We can only work together fruitfully to build a better world when we "lay all our cards on the table," rather than maneuver to get some kind of advantage over one another.

Totems

As a compulsed Three, I was like a *peacock*, demanding attention by strutting around, and making use of every little thing I could get for my own benefit.

As a redeemed Three, I have the new totem of the BALD EAGLE. Like the eagle I can be at ease with who I am. I have my place in society where perhaps I can achieve great things, but as peacefully and calmly as the flight of the great eagle. This is because I no longer have a compulsion to be successful. The bald eagle mates for life, and builds annually on its original nest. I, too, want to live in great loyalty to family and friends.

4. THE MISUNDERSTOOD FOUR[1]

Where Am I as a Four?

My Gifts

As a Four, anything that causes intense feeling attracts me, such as farewells, abandonment, cataclysmic happenings, and death itself. I am used to having emotional grief in my life. I know what it feels like to be misunderstood or abandoned. This has prepared me to be very sensitive to tragedy in the lives of others. I have a sixth sense for drawing into myself the feelings of others, even when I am not conscious of doing so. I naturally resonate with their emotions. This can be a burden, but I am able to use this vulnerability to back up another who is going through a crisis, and accompany a friend through a long road to recovery. As a heart person I have great *compassion*.

I am also very sensitive to the *aesthetic*. I absorb the beautiful into my soul and it makes me feel more fulfilled. I have an affinity with symbolic expression, which communicates on a deeper level than words can convey. This figures in the way I shape my immediate environment. I like to put the stamp of my good taste in the decor of my room or my house, so that anyone coming in will notice right away my originality.

Even more important to me is the *charm* of my person itself. I want my being to be naturally expressive of

---

[1] Cf Beesing, et. al., pp. 11, 27-30, 67-72, 104, 109, 117, 122, 133f, 141, 151, 170f, 173f, 185f, 196,207, 214f.

what my life has been. I want to give to others with elegance and originality the special gift that I am.

My Childhood

As a Four, I probably had feelings of *abandonment* as a child. There was some kind of personal tragedy which occasioned feelings of loss. Did a parent die? Was I simply abandoned or unloved? Did a parent frequently come in and go out of my life? Was I born into a grieving family and expected to identify with the loss an adult was suffering?

Whatever the childhood loss was, it has given me a sense of personal tragedy. Maybe I have even had recurring depression. At any rate, some loss has deeply marked my life and made it very different from others. No one can understand me without appreciating what I have gone through. Already in my childhood I felt misunderstood and somehow *different*.

My Pride

As a Four, I do not want to be psychologically labeled. I take pride in being very special and unique. I see myself surrounded by beautiful things that others do not seem able to appreciate the way I do. I see my heart uniquely attuned to life's joys and sorrows. I am a friend to nature, which I experience as fresh and simple and spontaneous. I like to think I am also that way, but then I get weighed down by loneliness and the loss I have had in my own life. I go back over the mistakes I made regarding some relationships, and get angry at myself because I can never change these mistakes I made.

Maybe I tend to be snobbish. If I look down on others it is just that I understand some things better than they do.

Time

Because of the weight of the past on my consciousness, it is sometimes difficult for me to live in the present moment. Because of lost opportunities I feel my past left me unfulfilled, and yet I have the need to ponder more deeply and re-live some of the emotional experiences I have had. I have lots of nostalgia.

My sense of time is subjective. It depends on my emotional experience. Time drags when I am not involved with my feelings, but it flies when I am. Then I tend to lose track of time, and this can make me late for an appointment. Should I be anticipating a deep experience of feeling, such as the arrival or departure of someone special, I will be on hand way ahead of time.

Talking Style

Since the symbolic is so important to me, I study my personal style, sometimes even rehearsing beforehand what I will say and how I will say it. I have a craving to be natural and spontaneous, but I am often painfully aware that I never seem to attain the simplicity and casualness I want to have. Others may see me as having a *studied charm*.

There is something of the *theatrical* in my nature. Sometimes it seems like I am acting out a role before others, and that life itself is like a performance on stage. I do love the theater, but while attending a play I find myself identifying more with the acting rather than being absorbed in the story as a vicarious experience. I love acting because of my need to express in an original way my most profound feelings.

I am always seeking the right style in what is special about me. At times I over-dramatize myself as a way to compensate for my lack of self-esteem. Others tend to think that I am somewhat *unreal* as a person and that I display more feeling than is actually in my heart, but they may be thinking that way because they lack my refinement. I use clothes to express my special refinement in a way that is understated but nevertheless exquisite.

Avoidance

As a Four, I avoid being *ordinary*. It is very important for me always to be seen as special, for I feel I am very different from other persons. My feelings are very unique. Others do not understand my feelings because they have not gone through what I have experienced.

Melancholy

The attraction I have to dwelling on feelings of *melancholy* gives a certain intensity to how I interpret my life. Past tragedies seem very dramatic to me. I tend to go back over the unhappiness of my past, such as my feelings of being abandoned, misunderstood, lonely, or having missed opportunities. I find my life rather mysterious, even to myself.

I have a lot of mood swings, but I feel most alive when I experience deep feelings, whether of joy or sorrow. I tend to live at the extremes of the spectrum of emotions, such that I can swing quickly from depression to hyperactivity as my moods change. Sadness, however, can get me down, so that I am not good for anything but shedding tears.

Pining

As a Four, there is a lot of yearning in my life for what is absent. My attention focuses on what is missing. Particularly I pine for a fulfilling relationship of love. What I experience at present tends to be dull in comparison with these longings. It seems that I have not yet begun to live, that my true self has not yet been awakened. Consequently it may be difficult for me to focus on actual events that are happening, and I tend to see in them their negative aspects.

Fantasizing

I do a lot of fantasizing about what is presently unavailable to me. My imagination tends to make up for whatever is lacking in the fulfillment of my desires. Often I feel more intimate with someone at a distance than when that person is close at hand. When I get depressed because of my own excessive self-criticism, I readily engage in thoughts of suicide. Even though it is unlikely I have ever intended actually to kill myself, I do see suicide as a dramatic way of dying.

Hyper-sensitivity

As a Four, I need to recognize that I tend to be *hyper-sensitive*. Others may be bewildered that I take things so personally, and that I feel so hurt by what others might consider just a social oversight, such as a friend missing my birthday, but that is just the way I am.

Self-pity

As a Four, I need to guard against self-pity, for I will tend to use it to draw attention to myself and even to establish a relationship with another person. There is a danger of my drawing another into my own unhappiness as a way of bonding with that person. Getting absorbed in myself by self-pity can become an obstacle in my relating with others, for it can cause others to have difficulty in getting close to me as an intimate friend.

Fulfillment

I see my fulfillment in the authentic expression of my unique feelings. To enhance the sense of my personal worth, I withdraw from others and practice how to be more authentic and original in the way I express myself. As I strive for fullness of life, I keep trying to express symbolically the special feelings I have within myself.

I have a craving for deep feelings. To feel neutral is for me to be only half alive. Often it seems that my real life has not yet begun, because I have not entered deeply enough into my feelings. As I see it, my emotional needs come before everything else. Sometimes it seems that the world is leaving me behind, while I am waiting for an experience of real life with others.

Preferred Center

As a Four, I am a heart person. I keep asking myself how others are responding to me. I live on a feeling level, and since my wing is in the head center, I also live somewhat in my thinking center. I will tend, however, to be lacking in my instinctive life, which pertains to the spontaneity of my gut center. I substitute my feelings for instincts.

Instead of letting spontaneity happen from instinct, I try to make myself have certain instinctive reactions in order to dramatize my life. Consequently, others experience my behavior as somehow put on, and this makes it difficult for others to read me from my self-expression. Without fully realizing it, I have put on an artistic mask over my bodily movements.

Where Do I Want To Go as a Four?

Not Moving with the Arrow

As a Four, I want to avoid moving with the arrow to take on also the compulsion of the ego-flattery Two. This would compound my compulsiveness. If I keep going over and over again in my heart a missed opportunity which I feel was my only hope to happiness, I may isolate myself and then entice a companion to share my isolation and despair. To cling to another out of desperation is really very unwise. If I am a true friend, I will bring the best of myself to the relationship. To build my life on the adage that "misery likes company" is to let my dark side take over for my friend and myself.

Moving Against the Arrow

To move toward greater freedom as a Four, I need to move against the arrow of compulsion by taking on the pride of the One, who says, "I am hard-working." Far from letting my feelings of discouragement cause me to withdraw from activity, I will grow in balance by taking on the *assertive behavior* characteristic of the One. Instead of lamenting about how tragic my life has been, I can grow healthier as a person by re-directing my criticism away from self and toward what is outside myself. I will always remain a Four, but I am able to lay aside my pride in being unique, and put in its place the pride of being hard-working. By taking on the idealism of the One, who works hard to improve the environment, I put into action the *power* of my refinement and other talents. My gifts can inspire and train others to develop their own creativity. By re-defining myself as a person dedicated to honesty, directness, and hard work, I will come to see how much I have to give others from what I already am.

Getting more involved will help me get in touch with my neglected gut center, which functions spontaneously by instinct in relationships. By making others deal with me and my values, I will become less moody and be more willing to take charge to get a job done. The idealism of the One can inspire me to see the importance of doing whatever is necessary to complete well whatever I begin. At the same time, my interaction with what I meet in the present will give me a better sense of reality, and I may even feel in my heart that I am a person on fire with my convictions.

From Traps to Holy Ideas

My trap as a Four was my idea of *authenticity*, which I thought I could achieve all by myself if I just got in touch with all that had happened to me, and kept practicing how to express myself before others. Dwelling on my past feelings with melancholy caused me to have a poor sense of the present moment and made me keep yearning for my real life to begin. Being so absorbed with myself made me somewhat unreal, and caused others difficulty in understanding me. I tended to put on the airs of "an aristocrat in exile." Without a conversion of heart, I probably would have continued never being quite myself.

For me as a Four, conversion involved replacing the trap of authenticity with the holy idea of UNION WITH GOD. Union with God begins with a yearning for God. This means I make of my life a journey to God. The classic image of this is that of climbing a mountain: Moses climbed Mt. Sinai, conversed with God face to face, and returned to the people with God's instructions to the people Moses was leading;[2] the prophet Elijah climbed that same mountain centuries later, encountered God, and returned with a clear focus and confidence to finish his life work;[3] Jesus himself climbed a high mountain, conversed with the apparitions of Moses and Elijah, and came back down the mountain readied to complete his work of salvation by his death and resurrection.[4] All three sought union with God as a means to overcome grave disappointments in their lives and work. They came to see that all their joys and sorrows fit into God's salvific plan: all was of use to God for working through them to fulfill what God planned to achieve on earth.

Union with God is not some feeling, or achievement, or the result of merit. It comes from understanding and intending that each experience I have is a means to my growing in union with God. I cannot meet God in the past or in the future. Because God exists only in the eternal now, I can encounter the holy mystery of God only in the now-moment. I have to learn to be open to the present moment if I am ever going to meet God face to face as did Moses, Elijah, and Jesus. To attain a sense of completeness as a person, I have to focus my attention on the present, reacting to it from my inner instinct, and appreciating

---

[2] Ex 19:20ff.

[3] 1 Kings 19:8ff.

[4] Mk 9:2ff.

whatever gifts it offers to me. In this way I can respond to God facing me in the present.

As I grow in union with God, I learn to recognize better that God has created me as a unique gift to others, just as God also is an unique Gift. All my past life can serve as a preparation for the response I make to what God's Providence presents to me right now. God's Providence has worked with all my past satisfactions and disappointments, that I would emerge as a irreplaceable and non-repeatable gift of God to others at this moment of history. My heart has been stretched by joys and squeezed by loss. Nothing that ever happened was simply ordinary. As I go on living in the flowing now of existence, I live in a series of unique moments made special by God's presence to me in each event as it occurs. I know I need to go on letting God shape me as a potter shapes a clay vessel,[5] for I am destined to contain an "eternal weight of glory."[6] This, for me as a Four, is to make abandonment to God my way of life.

From Passion to Virtue

As long as I lacked self-esteem and saw my fulfillment as an authentic, symbolic expression of myself, I was prone to compare myself with others who stood out as striking personalities. Their being special seemed to lessen who I was. Their giftedness seemed to pose a threat to my own giftedness, whether it was how I dressed, decorated my living quarters, or otherwise expressed myself. Instead of admiring them for their gifts, I would tend to belittle them. In a word, I was *envious*.

---

[5] Cf Jer 18:1ff.
[6] 2 Cor 4:17

Through holy abandonment to God, I will be able to move from this passion of envy to the virtue of *equanimity*. Instead of comparing my style with that of others, and wanting to draw the world's attention to myself as special, I can live in self-composure. I have my own special pathway to union with God through all the events unique to me in my life. Having recognized that all that happened has brought me closer to God, I focus on letting God continue to form me moment by moment according to my own destiny. I see myself being thus drawn into the mystery of life, where God dwells and unites together all our individual destinies. As St. Paul says, "...there is nothing in all creation that will ever be able to separate us from the love of God..."(Rm 8:39). What I had counted as lost opportunities were but some of the tough places I was going through as I climbed the mountain of God. I now believe that the open wounds, which have caused me so much anguish and sense of loss in my heart, will shine in glory as radiant scars of my soul, revealing the cross I carried as a follower of Jesus.

Totems

As a compulsed Four, I was like a *basset hound.* I expressed sadness as a way of establishing connection with others. My melancholy consisted in a collection of "sweet regrets," as I sat in sadness as a person very misunderstood.

Now, however, as a redeemed Four, I relate to the BLACK STALLION as my new totem. I feel I have the grace and free spirit of that animal in me. I walk tall, have a variety of gaits, come out to meet people when I wish to do so, and am ready to gallop away at any time with my mane tossing in the wind. I know I am a unique creation of a loving God, and I have the self-confidence that I can react instinctively to any situation in a way that expresses who and what I am. I recognize the good and beautiful when I see it, whether existing inside or outside myself.

5. THE ALOOF FIVE[1]

Where Am I as a Five?

My Gifts

As a Five, I find life full of meaning. I look for the deeper significance underlying what others might consider as ordinary events, and thus can help others appreciate much better what happens in their lives.

By nature I am non-critical. I recognize that it takes a long time to know anything, because there are many aspects that have to be grasped before one can make an adequate judgment. To me everything is interesting to know, so I do not start out by judging whether something is good or bad, right or wrong. Because of my non-judgmental attitude I can find humor in almost anything in a wry kind of way. My wit can pop up any time. I can make people laugh and feel less burdened in their lives.

When I communicate with others, it is very important to me that everything be understood. I try to boil down complex matters into simple and straightforward language. I am able to concentrate dispassionately on difficult problems, and to make good decisions when under pressure. Since I have a natural bent in planning long-range projects that demand vision, I am well-fitted as the brains behind a smoothly-running operation. When given authority I like to delegate responsibility and to encourage others to be self-reliant and make their own decisions.

---

[1] Cf Beesing, et. al., pp. 11f, 30-35, 72-78, 104, 108f, 117f, 122, 129f, 140, 152f, 167f, 174, 187f, 197, 207, 215.

I am also good at making lifelong friendships, provided my confidantes allow me the private space I need for myself. I am very good at expressing affection non-verbally, and at remembering with appreciation happy occasions of togetherness with another.

My Childhood

As a child, I sought opportunities to be by myself in places where others would not intrude. Perhaps I built a tree house just for myself. I enjoyed being by myself because solitary reflection and fantasizing satisfied a deep need I had to distance myself from involvement with other people. I may have had as company an imaginary playmate. Mayhap I felt as an abandoned orphan, unwanted by parents or guardians, or sensed being so different from the others in my family that I doubted I really was the offspring of my parents. Maybe, on the other hand, I sought to be alone because others had hurt me by the way they had intruded into what was private and personal to me. When I could not escape physically from others, I learned to distance myself psychologically. I kept outsiders from prying into my life by living inside myself in a way that kept them from knowing my thoughts or affecting my feelings.

My Pride

As a Five, it is important for me to withdraw from others in order to reflect and learn how everything fits together. I take pains to look at matters from every angle and to think things out for myself. I am proud about how much I know about some things that are really significant. As I see it, others are often superficial, or even positively stupid.

Time

As a Five, I watch time going by and reflect on what I see going on so as to understand its meaning. To me there is always something interesting that is happening, and if not outside myself then inside myself. Time is very precious to me, and I tend to be miserly with it, because there is never as much time available as I need for my projects that I am doing alone. I take pains to avoid getting caught in those social events which waste my time because they are not useful for learning something. Often I leave a social gathering unobtrusively as though I were invisible to everyone. I compartmentalize my life into time capsules, and then enter in turn into each time capsule without allowing my feelings to be engaged with the contents of my other time capsules.

Talking Style

People often complain that I am too quiet, as though my silence annoys them. I have a difficult time entering the flow of small talk, even though I may want to fit in with what others are saying. When I have finally thought out a remark to contribute to the conversation, I find that the others have already moved on to another subject. Sometimes when others are talking, I find myself tuning them out and attending to my own thoughts because my own inner world is more interesting. This poor sense of the present often causes me to forget names of persons to whom I have just been introduced.

As a Five, I have a tendency to speak too softly in conversation and to lack feeling in my speech. This is because I consider that what is important is the communication of my thoughts rather than my feelings. When others ask me how I feel about something I respond by telling them what I have been thinking. I am happy to share my thinking with others, but this does take some time, since what I have thought out includes a lot of details which I need to communicate clearly. Often it seems people find me difficult to listen to, as though what I am saying is boring to them. This makes me think others are too shallow to be interested in what I have come to know. As a result, I become more wary about sharing my inner world. After all, I see what I know as a treasure mainly for myself anyway: it is so important for me to understand as much as possible and thus be a wise person with correct judgment. Because I really prefer to be alone, when it is necessary to appear in public I develop strategies to draw attention away from myself, such as by talking in the other person's interest.

Avoidance

As a Five, there is in my life a fundamental desire to avoid people. I am reluctant to get involved with others, because I need time to be alone and I often have difficulty in sharing with others what I have been thinking about. There is this quest for a safe distance from others, whether it is by physical withdrawal or by avoidance of involvement. Since I compartmentalize my life, it is unlikely anyone will know how I am in all my time capsules, and others may find me evasive should they try to pry into my life. Since I very much dislike confrontation with others, my private space is my main self-defense, and that includes my withholding of information about myself.

Underlying my tendency to avoid people is my sense of inner *emptiness* which can be filled only if I am alone in seclusion. I have great concern to amass a storehouse of knowledge, and I fear to deplete my storehouse by sharing all I know about something. It is important for me to know much more than I ever share with others. Knowledge gives me the security of having acquired something that fills my inner emptiness.

I seek knowledge to prepare for the moment when my wisdom will be sought, so that I will not be caught foolish. I want to be forewarned and forearmed before I have to communicate what I know. Being unprepared is frightening to me because I do not want to be embarrassed. Since it takes a great deal of time to know anything well, I do not want to waste my time in situations that will not help me learn something significant.

Stingy

My ego-fixation is *stinginess*. I may argue that this is not so because I do not yearn for money and material possessions. Perhaps I prefer to do without material riches, or if I do have them, to live as though I am not wealthy. I need to recognize that stinginess is not the same as greed. Greed is lust to be wealthy; stinginess is reluctance to share what I have.

How, then, am I stingy as a Five? I want for myself the treasures I have acquired. Do I value my knowledge because others will benefit from it, or simply as a treasure which fills my inner emptiness? Am I not stingy with my time, avoiding doing services to others because I want that time for myself?

Aloof

My *aloofness* as a Five is probably much noticed by others. I avoid becoming involved with people and situations, lest I lose my freedom to pursue alone my private projects. There is also my aloofness of feeling. In encountering others I want to share my thinking but not my feelings. Either I do not want to express my feelings to others, or I am not able to do so because I am not in touch with how I feel. In any case, I think feelings are not very important. I tend to lack feelings because of my reluctance to get involved with events and undertakings that would elicit strong emotions.

I feel very uncomfortable as a Five trying to make small talk at parties. Perhaps I want to belong to groups and be part of social life, but this is draining on me and often makes me feel inferior to others. I become really alive when I am alone. The way for me to fit in with groups is to know the agenda of the meeting and to prepare ahead of time what I am going to say. Please do not expect me to socialize after the meeting. When the agenda is completed I am anxious to go home.

There is also an aloofness in the way I acquire knowledge and right judgment. I need to do this independently of others. I do not like to be supervised by another. To fill my inner emptiness I need to think things out on my own. Since I do not look for approval from others in order to feel good about myself, I can live happily in the company of my own private pursuits. I may feel best when I am emotionally unconnected to others.

Observing Reality

My aloofness and aloneness as a Five does not prevent me from knowing what is going on. I am a keen observer of reality. Although I may seem quite withdrawn from others, I do take pains to know and understand what is going on. I reflect on it and store it inside because I do not want to be stupid. I may walk into a gathering, sit down, and later walk out as though others do not notice me. Even when participating in a group, I may suddenly take leave without saying good-bye to anyone, simply because it is time for me to be alone again.

Fulfillment

Since I have denied my instinctive functioning, preparation for any action or reaction is supremely important to me as a Five. Such preparation is by perceiving and reflecting ahead of time. My chosen defense against a world making demands on me is knowledge that I have acquired while by myself. By withdrawing from others to be a intellectual observer of everything I believe I can stay on top of the world. This, then, is how I see my fulfillment: *to be is to be all-knowing.*

As a Five, then, I have chosen as absolute good the knowledge I can acquire by my own efforts while alone. This, I hope, will lead me to correct judgment about everything, and I will know how to fit into reality as it is.

This absolute I seek can never be attained. Since I will never have the time to know everything about everything, there will always remain within me a sense of emptiness or ignorance that can cause me to be restless in my craving to possess whatever time and solitude I can garner for myself. If I do not have solitude I will feel I am losing my life.

As a Five, I will be attracted to learning universal principles which explain the world, and especially those which help me understand human behavior. To be able to explain types of human personality and how people react to one another will give me equipment in my head center to fit in with others, without necessarily getting involved with my feelings. With such knowledge I can watch and understand others without losing control of all that protects me from the intrusions of others into my life. As a Five, I really am a guarded person. The reality of life is very interesting to watch, but it may be too frightening for me to participate in it.

Preferred Center

As a Five I have deliberately chosen my head center as that which is most important in being a person. This means that when I go into a new situation my first concern is how I will fit in. For me to fit in, I need to know the situation and how all its parts interrelate. I will tend to put myself in place of others to understand where they are. My attention focuses on where others are in the total situation, not how they relate to me. It is in this way that I seek control. Without needing any feedback from others, I rely on my own perception and reflection to understand the total situation. If I think I am okay, then I conclude I am okay. After any experience I will go over in my own mind how I was with the others, and decide how I will comport myself the next time I am in the same situation.

Since I have a wing in my heart center, I have a kinship with relationships built on feeling. I have a great problem, however, from having neglected my gut center, my instinctive functioning. Most likely this has been evident in sports, where gut reactions are so necessary for excellence. My use of my head center in sports' activities causes my response to be slow and reflective, instead of spontaneous. This has tended to make me self-conscious whenever I have tried to play ball with others.

Using my head center as my preferred way of functioning causes me to be very deliberate in my actions and reactions. By using my thinking function when instincts should be performing, my actions may appear rigid and mechanical. In emergency situations I am apt to freeze because functioning from my head center means I have to prepare my reaction by first reflecting, and that takes time that I do not have in an emergency. Fear simply paralyzes or debilitates me, rather than leads to a strong protective action. Any unexpected demand from others that I perform before a group when I have not prepared immediately beforehand causes me to panic inside.

Where Do I Want To Go as a Five?

Not Moving With the Arrow

As a Five, I will compound my problem by moving with the arrow of compulsion towards the ego-planning Seven. This would lead me to withdraw from reality and dwell on pipe dreams. I already have a compulsion to withdraw in order to reflect, and I will compound that compulsion if my reflections become pure fantasy. This could happen out of a dislike for my environment, or simply because of old age, such that I let my aloofness so isolate me that I live almost completely in my inner world and contemplate projects that I will never realize. It may also happen by choosing a research project that is so esoteric and complex that it will not serve anyone.

It is simply unhealthy for me as a Five to make plans which I can never put into action. My mind may be full of ideas, but I need to keep my feet on the ground, and use my ability to plan only those projects that I will be able to complete. My talents are for improving the world, not for a selfish satisfaction of daydreaming in solitude.

Moving Against the Arrow

As a Five, the enneagram can help me a great deal by telling me to move against the arrow of compulsion to the pride of the Eight, who says, "I am powerful." As a Five, I am liberated through taking the attitude of being a powerful person before others. Instead of being fearful of not being prepared to face a new situation, I need to insert myself into action before others, relying simply on the resources I have within myself. This is to live with personal assertion and self-communication. It is to say, "Here I am; deal with me!" To be assertive or even aggressive will not feel right to me as a Five, but by trusting in the enneagram theory of moving toward the personality of the Eight I will discover a greater sense of fulfillment. I may want to withdraw again for reflective preparation characteristic of the Five, but I need to know that my call to be a person will always involve putting myself forward in any group I am in, so that others receive the gift of my presence and resources.

It is this taking on the assertiveness of the Eight that can overcome my inclination as a Five to feel inadequate in facing fresh challenges of life. My Fiveness tends to make me afraid of getting involved in life, whereas Eights thrive in facing such challenges. As a Five, I have the ability to take on that self-confidence, for I really do have great inner resources. Like Peter I need to have the guts to try walking on the water when I am invited to do so, as if the Lord is saying to me: "Come on out; the water is fine."[2] This could mean for me to take leadership in a new situation even when I have not had time for preparation. I may discover that I do have gut instincts on which I can rely. Just as Jesus asked Peter why he doubted when walk-

---

[2] Mt 14:27.

ing on the water, I too am called to self-confidence when acting by my instincts. With perseverance I can take on a personality that really enjoys life as an adventure, and not be so afraid of getting hurt or humiliated.

By trusting the inner wisdom of my instinctive center, and making others deal with me, I will become much more creative. Such living out of my gut center is like opening up an interior spring. At first the water is muddy, but as it flows out it gradually becomes crystal clear. Similarly, my efforts to be impulsive,—doing things in front of others with little or no preparation,— may at first be awkward and embarrassing; eventually, however, I will become more trusting in my spontaneity and the results may be much more satisfying for myself and others. This strengthening of the "muscles" of my instinctive center will gradually give me a better sense of myself and confidence in being a person of action. I will see I am stretching myself to live also on the gut level, where I react spontaneously to the words and actions of others, or cause them to react to me. I will be able to see also that I am really sharing the gift I am in ways that can benefit others. By getting in touch with my inner well by action, I may find in myself a new boldness, an ardent zeal to challenge the world.

From Traps to Holy Ideas

As a Five, I am trapped by my idea of *knowledge*, which I think I can attain all by myself through withdrawing for study and reflection. Such pursuits lead me into aloofness from others, since I see others as a distraction,— and even a hindrance,—to my having the time and private space to reach fulfillment. I crave solitude as the way I fill up my emptiness and prepare for the actions I am planning to take.

I tend to equate my own thinking with what others call "experience," and when others ask how I feel I reply by saying what I have been thinking about. This can cause me to have weak interpersonal relationships, and because of a kind of shyness which disappoints others who want excitement in social life. Without a conversion of heart I probably will never overcome the aloofness which characterizes my personality as a Five. This conversion, however, can be triggered by replacing my trap of knowledge with the holy idea of DIVINE PROVIDENCE.

Divine Providence means that God acts in our lives to take care of all our needs. Included in these needs is the knowledge we need to function well. By my abandonment as a Five to God's Providence, I trust that through events in my life God will make available to me whatever preparation I need for the actions I will be taking. I need to notice what comes in the mail, or what others tell me, as possible resources offered to me for what I will be doing. Furthermore, in the action itself I can count on divine assistance. This idea of Providence will release me from the notion that my ultimate good is knowledge, that it is only by self-attained knowledge that I will be fulfilled.

Such an abandonment to Providence amounts to an intellectual conversion for me as a Five. I am invited to make a leap of faith, trusting in a practical way that God will provide for all my needs in order to get involved and to function well. I will let life itself be my teacher.

As a Five, I have often said to others in the secret of my heart: "Let me alone." Now that I let go of the fears and timidity which hinder me from social involvement, I may discover that others in casual ways teach me knowledge I could never find in books. After all, many books are written by Fives who are uninvolved in what they analyze.

There is a wisdom written within human hearts which can hardly be learned from books. The greatest knowledge is that derived from *mystery*, namely, reality which can be known only by being personally involved in it. No amount of definitions can teach me what love really is if I myself am not personally involved with others. I can hardly know the mystery of death unless I have been at the bedside of a dying loved one. I can know the mystery of hope only by having fallen into a predicament where I had to rely on powers outside of my own resources to save me.

There is a knowledge I can attain only by living in this present moment of history, and can never gain merely from stories of the past. Instead of thinking of what is happening now in people as only a fad, or something to be *named*, as I may do to remain aloof, I need to be part of the human aspirations being enkindled by God's Spirit throughout the world in this moment of history. This is to live by discerning "The Signs of the Times." Is there not a common underground spring feeding the deep wells of many persons in a given moment of time? Through involvement with "the joys and the hopes, the griefs and the anxieties of the people of this age,"[3] I find I am called to live a shared life in a shared world, accepting my creaturehood as a call to communion with my fellow creatures.

From Passion to Virtue

Before I took the step of abandoning myself to Providence, I felt I was losing my life unless I had the solitude I needed to store up knowledge within myself. I did

---

[3] Vatican II, Pastoral Constitution on the Church in the Modern World, art. 1. Concerning the term "signs of the times,' Cf Ibid., art. 4.

not see I needed involvement with another to attain my fulfillment. This was obvious from the resentment I felt when a friend would intrude into my private space or take away the time I had planned for myself. Since I always felt empty and ignorant inside, I craved to possess whatever time and solitude I could get for myself. This made me stingy with my time and I was careful to avoid commitments which would entangle me in duties for and with others. For me real life began when I could be alone with my projects.

My accepting the holy idea of Providence as my way of abandonment to God can move me from the passion of stinginess to the virtue of *detachment*. This means that I am disposed to live off the gifts of life day by day, instead of the craving to store up resources for future eventualities. By accepting life itself as my teacher, and letting myself become committed and involved, I give up clinging to my own privacy. Because I am able to trust God's Providence, it becomes less necessary to find security for future action by storing up resources of knowledge. It also becomes easier for me to share my own inner world in personal encounter, because I now know that the mystery of life is lived in personal communion. In personal communion I find my soul being changed by taking on qualities and attitudes of those I love.

As a result of all this, I now recognize that being self-sufficient is not the virtue I thought it was. It may even be, in fact, a vice. What is most important is the knowing of persons, a knowledge acquired only by investing myself in relationships. I have become grateful to God for sending me persons who love me enough to draw me out of my cave, and keep saying to me that they want me to share with them the worlds I have inside myself. They also invite me to share the worlds they have inside themselves I have come to believe in love itself as giving a fulfillment far surpassing whatever fulfillment I could attain by my own study and reflection cut off from others.

Totems

As a compulsed Five, my totem was the *fox*. Like a fox I had an intense gaze, and knew what was happening around me because I watched it. My den was my private space in solitude where I always had a lot to do, whether to amuse myself or to pursue some ambitious project all alone. I would often slink around on the edge of social life, and tackle only small projects that would not involve me in lasting commitments or great publicity.

As a redeemed Five I have a new totem: the OWL. Like an owl I have a public presence which is alert and self-composed. No longer am I plagued by inner fears and self-doubt when taking an initiative before others. I recognize I have power to see deeply into complex situations, and I feel like a skilled chess player as I confront my adversaries, who may mistake my gentleness for timidity and weakness. I am confident of my timing and skill in dealing successfully with all antagonists. Like an owl I know I have the re-sources to overcome my opponents, even though they may be bigger and stronger than I am.

6. THE APPREHENSIVE SIX[1]

Where Am I as a Six?

My Gifts

My major gifts as a Six are my loyalty and my sense of responsibility. I am ready to sacrifice myself in dedication to my group, and I am willing to suffer with others as we work for a cause, even against tremendous odds. I do not need a lot of recognition from others in order to work hard with our group or team. Whatever problem our group may face, I will feel it a duty to work through the problem to get it resolved.

People notice my punctuality and the fact that I do not mind working overtime as long as my boss knows I am doing so. Because I can be very responsible and devoted to a group, I can also function well as its leader or boss, provided that there are appropriate and clear guidelines.

My Childhood

Already as a child I lived in *apprehension*. For some reason I felt unprotected and vulnerable. I may have been raised very strictly, so that I was insecure and afraid to make decisions for myself. Maybe my parents were disturbed themselves, and sometimes took out their frustrations by punishing me. As a child, I watched adults so as to be able to predict how they would act. By conforming to the demands and even suggestions of others, I could know how to protect myself from being embarrassed or hurt. Because I knew my own security or goodness depended on conforming

---

[1] Cf Beesing, et al., pp. 12, 35-40, 79-84, 103, 112, 118, 122f, 131, 138f, 153-155, 164f, 174f, 188f, 197, 208, 216.

to their wishes, I had to check out what others intended before making a decision.

My Pride

As a Six, I take pride in being loyal to a group. I want others in the group, especially those in authority, to see me as a faithful member of the group. To be a good person I believe I must fulfill all the external duties demanded of me by the laws and regulations coming from some authority. I enjoy being told what I am supposed to do and even how I am to do it.

Time

As a Six, I want to use all my time in a responsible way. If I do not know what is demanded of me, I will be uncertain as to what to do. This makes it difficult for me to know what to do with free time. Since time measures my responsibilities, it is not my own possession. In order to avoid getting into trouble, I see to it that I get my work done on time. I do my work with dispatch because that way I will make less mistakes. I will be punctual not only in arriving but also in leaving. I let the clock run my life.

Avoidance

Because I see life as governed by laws, rules and norms, I am an apprehensive person. Out of responsibility to the demands that life makes on me and on others, I see it as very important that we avoid *deviance*. I am very sure of myself when insisting that we observe the norms and regulations of the group we belong to, especially when these come from an authority figure or are put down in writing. I see life as consisting in the performance of one's duties. Although at times I myself may break the rules of the group to which I belong, I do not like to admit this even to myself because I think any deviance is really wrong.

Self-doubt

As a Six I am troubled by *self-doubt*. I generally feel insecure. I do not want to make a mistake in my decisions and I am afraid I will do so. This makes me very cautious. Others find me reluctant to act or to complete what I have started. A reason it is difficult for me to move from planning to action is that I see so readily what might go wrong. Since I tend to be afraid to act on my own, I have a problem with finishing what I begin. I often hesitate and procrastinate because I question my own capacities to do a task. Even success itself does not take away my fears, since others may not like what I do. I may cover up my uncertainty either by hyperactivity or else by doing absolutely nothing. I am not a self-starter; I work much harder when I receive direction from the outside.

Apprehensive

I feel *apprehensive* because to me life is full of demands and dangers. Many of these demands come from the group to which I belong. The dangers may come from any quarter. Often what I fear is simply the unknown, such as the uncertain future. I need to know the worst that might happen so as to prepare myself, but I don't usually try to imagine the best that might happen. I have a fear of change. I feel safer keeping to the tried and true of the past, rather than experiment by trying something new.

Indecisive

Others often find me *indecisive*. Other people's objections tend to make me nervous and hesitant about my own opinions. I feel I have to be very cautious about making any decision which will result in major changes, lest I make a mistake.

Overly-serious

As a Six, I have a real bent to being *overly-serious*. In part this is because I feel so responsible about the demands made on me. It is also because I feel things may very well turn out badly. I do not have much of a sense of humor because I am preoccupied by many possible dangers. Being so serious, I tend to postpone pleasures.

Legalistic

What particularly preoccupies me as a Six are the demands made on me by authority. I see life governed by laws, regulations, norms, and even simply by whatever is set down in writing. I feel we all need clarity in what is right and what is wrong and that this is to be defined by an authority. I tend to be *legalistic*, that is, I make obedience to laws an end in itself, rather than a means to an end.

In matters of morality and religion I tend to judge myself and others mainly on the outward observance of laws and accepted traditions. I identify with those faithful to laws and traditions. Here I often see life in terms of "them" and "us." Even though there may be few of *us* left, we are convinced we are superior to *them* in faithfulness and uprightness. I tend to be suspicious of *their* intentions and, for this reason, may misjudge *them*.

Fulfillment

As a Six I have a self-concept that I must conform to the world as it is in order to be a worthwhile person. My self-worth is dependent on carrying out the responsibilities given me from the outside. For me, *to be is to be responsible*. This fulfillment is something that is received. I must satisfy the demands made on me. In this way I can be in harmony with what is outside me.

Since I experience life as constantly making demands, I feel I am in contact with life only when I am apprehensive about failing to fulfill what is expected of me. Apprehensiveness keeps me focused on my own fulfillment; it keeps me concerned about all my responsibilities. Were I not apprehensive, I probably would be failing to face up to what life requires of me.

Since security is a big issue with me, I seek it by loyalty to an outside authority which I obey. I look for an authority outside myself to give me a direction in life, to tell me what I can do and cannot do, and set limits. It is by carrying out these norms as duties that I acquire and maintain my self-worth.

Preferred Center

As a Six, I have chosen my head center as the way to be a person, much to the detriment of the functionings proper to the heart center and the gut center. As a head person I keep asking, "How does all this go together?" Instinctively I focus on the total situation and how all its parts fit together. With this information I will know how to be in the situation. My instinct is not first of all to focus on relating personally with others as a heart person would do, nor do I boldly enter into the situation and plant myself there as a gut person would do. I must first size up the situation, and then I will know how to fit in.

In this sizing up of the situation, my instinct is to put myself in the place of others rather than ask how I am relating to them. By my thinking function I reflect on how other individuals are in regard to the total situation. I do not rely on others to tell me that I am okay; my own perceptions tell me that. Like a Five, after the experience I will think it over again reflectively to plan how I will act the next time I am in that situation.

Living as I do in my head, I find my security in knowledge, but this knowledge must not change. As a result, I am reluctant to do serious reading. New knowledge could cause conflicts with what I already know, and this would be threatening to my inner security. I cling to knowledge based on what in the past has given me security. To me the rules governing my life are not supposed to change. Paradoxically, I have chosen my thinking function as the ideal way to be a person, and yet I fail to use my head to know reality in the changing situation in which we live today.

My basic problem as a Six begins with my preferred center, but it also extends itself in the way I use my thinking center to substitute for my feeling function (the heart center) and for my instinctive function (the gut center). As regards feeling, instead of relating to people heart to heart, I make my love of them a matter of fulfilling my duties. I will tend to show my love toward my children mainly by my good example and by providing their material necessities, rather than feel I need to show love by the expression of affection and intimate conversation. Here, then, I use my head center to substitute for matters proper to the heart center.

As regards my body movements, which should be instinctively expressed by my gut center, I will tend instead to govern them also by my head center. People find me much more rigid than flexible even in the way my body is present to a situation. Since I have chosen to use my head center to govern my being and its conduct, I have a cautious deliberateness in my movement, which is very different from someone who is spontaneous and outgoing.

Where Do I Want To Go as a Six?

Not Moving With the Arrow

In times of stress as a Six, when I feel very indecisive or threatened by others, I may cover over my self-doubt with a feigned conviction of certitude in a way that others find intimidating. By stubbornness I try to control others in a passive-aggressive way by not cooperating with them. On the other hand, I may decide that the best approach to danger is in taking a strong offense, and I bad-mouth any opposition to my group as of malicious intentions to be denounced in the name of the law. This may lead me to experience restlessness, such that I am unable to sit still and be innerly centered.

What I have done is to compound my compulsion as a Six by moving with the arrow of compulsion toward the ego-vanity Three. Threes are very decisive and very active. They move out to others in an assertive and even aggressive way, presenting what they are promoting even with a feigned sincerity. As a Six, I may even seek to escape my insecurity by placing myself in a very dangerous endeavor where the pressure to survive will cause me to focus all my attention on gaining the glory of victory over my opponent.[2]

Moving Against the Arrow

Instead of moving with the arrow to the compulsion of the Three, I will gain greater wholeness in my instincts as the Six by moving against the arrow of compulsion toward the pride of the Nine, who says, "I am content." As a Six I need the inner quietude of the Nine. This demands of me that I learn to live within my gut center as I move into a situation. Instead of saying, "How do I fit into the total situation?" I need to take pride in just being myself, and let people deal with me in my bodily presence. I need the confidence of the Nine that I will be okay as a person just by letting myself be in the situation I am in at present. This includes having the Nine's instinctive attitude that all that is really important is peace and harmony between individuals and within our own selves.

This calls for me to reform my conscience. Instead of considering that morality is a matter of rules and laws, of conformity to external authority, I need to accept a morality based on what are called *values*. Jesus expressed this in his sermon against the hypocrisy of the Scribes and Pharisees, as in Mt. 23. In spite of all their scrupulous attentions to the minutiae of the Law, they neglected to obey the really important teachings of the Law, such as justice, mercy, and honesty (v. 23). As he says, they strain out a gnat from their drink but swallow a camel (v. 24).

---

[2] Cf Helen Palmer, *THE ENNEAGRAM. Understanding Yourself and the Others in Your Life,* Harper, San Francisco, 1988, pp. 244f.

As a Six, do I disrupt my harmony with some people because I exaggerate the importance of external conformity to some authority? If so, why do I see that external conformity as more important than getting along with others? Why do I instinctively exaggerate the importance of certain rules of external conduct in myself and others to the detriment of the greater value of peace? I need to let go of making external norms as ends in themselves, as the be-all and end-all of what is right and wrong. As St. Paul says, "we must always aim at those things that bring peace and help strengthen one another."[3] It is within my capability to let go of my compulsive conscience and take on the laid-back conscience of the Nine. I can take pride in being "easy-going" and being a peacemaker. It may not feel right, but I can learn to live out of my neglected gut function. By moving toward the pride of the Nine I will never become a real Nine, but my personality as a Six will become more healthy, more approachable, and more *spontaneous.*

From Traps to Holy Ideas

As a Six, I am trapped by my idea of *security,* a security which I fail to find within myself, but instead seek to attain by conformity to an outside authority. Since I always feel someone is looking over my shoulder, I am over-cautious and lack self-confidence. I experience life as full of demands. People find me excessively serious and apprehensive. I am dependent on being acceptable within my own group by conforming in my external behavior to its norms and traditions.

Since I focus so much on external conformity, I tend to be judgmental of those who deviate from group

---

[3] Rm 14:19.

norms, and self-righteous in regard to my own loyalty. I so identify my own self with the norms of my group that I consider any attack on those norms as a personal attack against myself. While outwardly professing perfect conformity to law and rules, I may clandestinely act contrary to these norms without acknowledging this before others or even to myself, and live a double life without remorse of conscience. In this way, I may make a caricature of true religion and morality as mere external observance rather than a permanent disposition of one's inner being.

I can be freed from this trap of security by the holy idea of TRUST IN GOD. Instead of being dependent for ultimate security on conformity to the norms of my group, I abandon myself to God in trust of God's parental love for me as God's own child. My security now stems not from what I do, but from what God has done through Jesus Christ in the Holy Spirit to bring me forth into a new birth of water and the Spirit, whereby as an adopted child I share the inheritance of God's first-begotten Son. This means that at last I can be radically safe because of who I am, God's child, rather than because of the good works of obedience I have done. This is to glory in God and in the divine work of salvation, rather than to glory in my good works, which, I must confess, often have caused me to exalt myself as better than others.

Much of the writing of St. Paul concerns this intellectual conversion as rooted in the salvation worked by Jesus, which I am called to accept. I now can understand what Paul meant when he wrote that "we are put right with God only through faith, and not by doing what the Law commands."[4] The reason for my right relationship with

---

[4] Rm 3:28.

God, and my consequent eternal salvation, is the work of God through Jesus Christ by means of which I have become an adopted child of God. Good parents always love their children before their children respond in love to them. In the same way, my union with God is based on a communion of love initiated by the Father toward me through Jesus Christ. I am loved with the same parental love with which the Father loves Jesus Christ.[5]

The way to please God, as to please any good parent, is to recognize and accept the parental love in awe, gratitude, and responding filial devotion. With this faith, then, I understand that I can easily receive pardon for any deviance on my part. My misdeeds are not necessarily a cause for losing salvation. All that really can cause that loss is to place my ultimate security in something other than God's parental love for me.

By living an inner-directed religion in this way, I will experience a freedom from anxieties that may have haunted me since I was a child. With St. Paul I can accept that "there is nothing in all creation that will ever be able to separate us from the love of God which is ours through Christ Jesus our Lord."[6] I will cease to watch the conduct of others so judgmentally, for having sensed God's unconditional love for me as an adopted child, I can sense also that same unconditional love God has for my neighbor, whatever that person's conduct. Since my religion has now come to mean that I imitate God's ways, I want to love that person with that same unconditional love. It seems strange it has taken me so many years to understand this basic Christian message!

---

[5] Cf Jn 17:26.
[6] Rm 8:39.

From Passion to Virtue

Before I abandoned myself to God's parental love in absolute trust of God, I felt much anxiety and apprehension deep within my being. I could never be sure of being accepted as a worthy person, because I was afraid of being seen as not fulfilling my duties. This especially plagued me with fear when I was uncertain as to what was right and what was wrong. Although all my life I had been living in the midst of rapid social change, my own security required the avoidance of change in laws and customs. Anything that overturned the customary way of doing things could be for me a real threat to inner peace. Because I found life so full of demands, I was overly serious and did not allow myself much in the way of pleasure and frivolity. My own fear of making a mistake sometimes paralyzed me so that I put off making needed decisions. Fear was my constant companion in life.

My conversion by abandonment to God, through the holy idea of Trust in God, relaxes me and causes many of my previous fears to vanish. I am getting used to being a courageous person. This courage comes from the security of my divine adoption. As St. Paul writes, "If God is for us, who can be against us?"[7] Changing customs and optional regulations become less threatening to me even within my own religious tradition, because I see that the response God asks of me is never adequately indicated by what I do or do not do exteriorly. Rather than having a *judging* God who watches for my every misstep, I have a *parenting* God who draws me into new situations, like Jesus invited Peter to walk on the water with him one windy night.[8] Peter's de-

---

[7] Rm 8:31.
[8] Cf Mt 14:25-32.

cision to respond to that invitation was tentative and risky, and he failed to do it perfectly. All the same, he grew in faith by the experience that when he began to sink Jesus was right at his side.

This faith of Peter challenges me as a Six to take risks in trying new things which are not stipulated by any laws or institutions. Being free from the preoccupation caused by fear of doing wrong, I can trust more the spontaneity of my own gut center to give me the courage to make of my life an adventure. Perhaps in the past I did not acknowledge the *cowardice* that was my natural disposition, or "passion." It is good for me to recognize that as a Six I have more opportunities than others to grow in *courage* because I have had so much practice in overcoming fears.

Totems

As a compulsed Six, I used to live like a scared *rabbit*. I felt extremely vulnerable. In the face of danger, I would panic rather than gather my forces in defense. I was very apprehensive because I was so unsure of myself.

As a redeemed Six, I have been given the DEER as my new totem. My alertness is now not anxious but relaxed. I stay close to others as deer do with one another, but my security is mainly within myself. I trust that God fondly loves me for who I am, and this gives me a confidence that at a moment's notice I can spot danger and gracefully leap to safety. I am not preoccupied with preparing for the worst in order to survive. Life is much more enjoyable than that. No matter what dangers may stalk me, I know that I am always under divine protection because *I belong to God.*

7. THE SANGUINE SEVEN[1]

Where Am I as a Seven?

My Gifts

As a Seven, I am good-natured, sanguine, and jovial. I think of myself as having a very pleasant appearance. I want to enjoy life by filling my surroundings with good cheer. I promote good will and good fellowship. I like parties. I like to entertain others and emphasize what is good and positive. I believe life itself needs celebration. I help others to celebrate their persons and their accomplishments, and to be hopeful about their future. To me there is great joy just in expecting good times. When I am not laughing with others, I am at least smiling.

My Childhood

Probably I grew up in a warm family, and later suffered because this was taken away from me. As a result, I am always looking for a lost coziness. Should it have happened that my parents or teachers were threatening to me as a child, I learned to cope by trying to disarm them by my pleasant manner, or I escaped by imagining what was pleasant.

My Pride

I take pride in being a *nice person*. I approach others without guile or suspicion. For me to stand out as a

---

[1] Cf Beesing; et al., pp. 12, 40-42, 85-89, 103, 113f, 118f, 123, 133, 139, 155, 166, 175, 189f, 197f, 208f, 216f.

good person I need cheerful surroundings. I give my attention to the bright side of life, and I believe in enjoying the best life can offer.

Time

Since for me there is always a panoply of interesting things to do, time can be stretched to include all I want to happen. When I am having a good time, there is always more time to keep the fun going. I also live a lot in future time. Since I like making plans, I enjoy the future before it happens. I do tend to be late, but for me the enjoyment of what is happening is more important than watching the clock. I always keep a lot of options open on how I will use my time, just to keep life exciting.

Talking Style

As a Seven, I am a great talker. I like to tell stories about people just to entertain. People find me very outgoing and likable. I am hardly ever at a loss for words. I have no difficulty making small talk at social gatherings. I try to persuade everyone to have a good time. If something troubling comes along I find ways to talk my way out of it.

Avoidance

As a Seven it is very important for me to avoid tension and pain. I avoid unpleasant confrontation with others. I prefer to sweep conflict under the rug, rather than deal directly with it face to face. Because of my avoidance of tension, I do not like to give orders to my subordinates. I think we should all participate in our organization in our own way without bumping into one another.

Because I prefer to look at the bright side of life, I look away from the distress of others. When life becomes stressful I look for distraction by planning pleasant activities. To talk about my plans is almost as good as to carry them out.

Multiple Options

Because I want life to be adventurous, I prepare *multiple options*. Should one activity become uninteresting, I always have another one in my plans. I feel best when I am moving rapidly from one stimulating happening to another.

Superficiality

Some people think I am *superficial*. Friends find me avoiding one-on-one intimacy. My penchant for having multiple options makes me uncomfortable with intimacy and commitment. I like the cheerfulness of a crowd, — the more people the better. I want my charm to cover up what is in reality a flight from intimacy and engagement.

Perhaps my spouse was attracted to marrying me because of my natural charm, and then was disappointed in the lack of personal closeness between us. To me, friendship is mostly having a good time with others,—and the more the merrier,—rather than sharing heart-to-heart in private.

Planning

As a Seven my ego-fixation is *planning*. I think of reality as making plans. I keep looking to the future with delight because of the plans I have for interesting happenings with others. I make plans to maintain a high level of excitement in my life.

Procrastination

I have a tendency to *procrastination*. I like to put off whatever become tedious. When I get bogged down by details I tend to put them out of my mind by turning to do something more pleasant. This may disappoint those who were counting on me to carry out the task I agreed to do, but I maintain a pleasant demeanor through it all.

I want all of us to enjoy life. It is hard for me to be serious. I need to admit I often become over-enthusiastic in planning interesting things, and that what I accomplish may not come up to the expectations of myself and others.

Fulfillment

To feel really alive as a Seven, I need an environment full of good cheer. My self-worth depends on life around me being pleasant. I tend to look away from whatever is painful or laborious.

I seek fulfillment by moving toward others through having plans for future events. I put my energy into changing the environment so that life will be exciting. I make cheerfulness an absolute good, while closing my eyes to the distressful aspects of life. If I do not have pleasant experiences with others, I tend to think something is wrong with me.

Preferred Center

As a Seven, I am a head person, with a wing on my gut center. I seek control by knowing where everything fits in. I rely on my thinking and reflection to tell me how everybody is and where I fit in, without my needing to listen to any feedback from others. If I think I am okay, I know I am okay.

My heart center has been very neglected. I do not ask the question of whether or not others like me. I have a penchant for *projecting* on others how they are to feel. Since I am so warm and charming in a group setting, why do I flee from the greater warmth possible in intimacy? It is because I feel a need to be in control by using my head center in place of the functioning appropriate to the heart center. I relate to others by planning activities I will enjoy having with them, and I consider this is the way to celebrate close friendship. This surprises those who are attracted to me in a very personal way, since they would like to be alone with me. I keep in control by being a party person. I need to admit I do not know how to function well on a feeling level. I do not like to cuddle.

Because of my wing in my gut center, I am spontaneous in my interaction with others. It is noticeable, however, how I sidestep confrontation with others. I do not enjoy what real gut persons do when they boldly enter into a situation and demand that others deal with them. If I am a supervisor I will consider by job well done if I let everyone take their own initiative as participants in our organization.

Where Do I Want To Go as a Seven?

Not Moving With the Arrow

As a Seven, I seek fulfillment by adapting to the world as I see it by my optimism. I should admit, however, that others may have just as much reason for pessimism as I have for optimism. To take on the pessimism of another, however, would really compound my compulsions. It would lead me to follow the arrow of compulsion to the ego-resentment One, who is always dissatisfied about something.

Ones are always critically aware that the environment is not the way it should be. This pessimism could get hold of me as a Seven if I live in an environment or an organization that is constantly unresponsive to my value of celebrating life. As a result, resentment about what is outside me could make me angry and aggressively critical. This would dampen my natural *joie de vivre*. I would be letting myself get stuck in a critical attitude which keeps repeating itself like an old record. Even my best friends may then become outsiders or even enemies.

If I take on the ego-resentment of the One, I will experience darkness in my gut center because of my negative attitude. I will want to experience consolation but be unable to do so, and instead I will fantasize feelings of consolation in my head. I can put up a good front even before myself, but the dark pessimism will remain deeply imbedded in my soul, much to the distress of my friends.

Moving Against the Arrow

Instead of making myself psychologically unhealthy as a Seven by becoming antagonistic toward social reality because it is not responsive to my values, I need to move against the arrow of compulsion to take on the pride of the Five, who says, "I am knowing." Fives withdraw from social reality they find unfulfilling. To gain balance as a Seven, I need that wisdom of the Five. I need solitude in order to figure out what is good and bad about the world with greater objectivity. This will help me become empathetic rather than overly-critical. Solitude will help me develop my neglected heart center, so that I listen to the many voices of the outside world rather than *impose* my own attitudes, be that from my natural optimism or from a bitter pessimism stemming from moving with the arrow of compulsion into the ego-resentment of the One.

It is healthy for me as a Seven to take delight in knowing reality just as it is. By giving up my old pride of being nice, I can take on the pride of being a *knowing person*. Such knowing through private study and reflection will help me get in touch with my inner well of wisdom. By getting closer to myself I can also get closer to others, since my own depth calls forth the inner depth of others. I can acquire an intuitive sense of relating to others on a deep level. I will be able to be more a part of their lives and experience real oneness with them, however they are. Such empathy can elicit in me the spiritual joy of being with others, not only in their happy times but also in their sorrows.

This transition to the pride of the Five takes on a special form for me because I will always remain a Seven innately fond of people. I want to know people rather than theories, and I can do that by listening with the heart. Through this I will discover that just to be silent with another who is in grief can be a great satisfaction.

From Traps to Holy Ideas

To become free to grow spiritually as a Seven I need to face my addictive idea, or "trap," of *idealism*. I have been living too much in my head. I have made my life consist too much of talking and planning, rather than the engagement of myself. Instead of choosing love, I have been choosing escape. The time comes in my life when I need to give up the ways of the child and accept the responsibilities of an adult life, when having fun takes a back seat to the satisfaction of living in commitment. My penchant for always keeping my options open and that life be constant celebration needs to give way to a spirituality centered on hard work. Am I ready to accept the truth that we are called to realize our humanness by our work?

Jesus himself was an outgoing and cheerful prophet. He enjoyed a good meal and fellowship. Above all, however, he engaged himself in the work of salvation he was sent to accomplish, and that meant carrying a cross. He chooses us to carry on his work of transforming the world into God's Kingdom. In order to do this, however, we must follow the path Jesus chose. We have called this the holy idea of CO-CREATION. It involves taking on the divine message that God draws good out of evil. It is to live the "paschal mystery," accepting the Cross as the way to bettering the world. Jesus said it was like giving birth through labor pains.[2] The birth of new human life simply does not take place without pain. To work for the new life of the Kingdom of God we need to accept embracing the Cross. Using another metaphor, Jesus said we have to die to ourselves just as a seed dies in the earth before it can bring forth new life and bear fruit.[3]

As a Seven, abandonment to God will center on my carrying my daily Cross as following the footsteps of Jesus to Calvary.[4] This is the way I need to put love into action. Any good that I want to accomplish should be worth whatever price it costs me to bring it forth. I need to buckle down to the hard work of carrying out in detail the good I have planned to accomplish with others. Part of this will be to share the burdens of others who are in doubt, distress, or even despair. I will want to help others to live through their

---

[2] Jn 16:21f.
[3] Jn 12:24f.
[4] Lk 9:23ff.

trauma with the hope and conviction that God intends a great good to come out of any evil we suffer in trying to bring about good.

From Passion to Virtue

By abandoning myself to God through accepting and embracing the Cross as my personal spirituality, I can hope to be freed from the distortion of my affections. Instead of making a god of pleasure and excitement, I will grow to be much more earnest as a person. Such *sobriety* heals my passion of *over-indulgence*. What becomes important is not that an activity be pleasant but that it be fruitful. I can empathize with the soberness of others who work hard on their projects for human development.

Out of my desire to realize a good I envision, I can focus my energy on making it real, and this will can give me considerable satisfaction. Out of love for the good to be accomplished, I can appreciate and even love each detail to which I give my full attention as I carry out the project. I will learn also to limit my plans to what I am committed to achieving, rather than continue my old pattern of having multiple options.

Totems

As a compulsed Seven I was like a *monkey*, noisy and full of excitement, living up in the air. I mainly wanted life to be pleasant. I kept a multitude of activities going in my life and always was ready for more.

Now as a redeemed Seven, through my soberness in embracing the Cross I have been gifted with a new totem: the BUTTERFLY. The butterfly shows me that my new personality has emerged out of a long period of darkness and struggle within myself. I recognize that just as a butterfly reflects the sun's light by its wings, so I want to radiate God's love and beauty by my presence. As the butterfly is attracted to the beauty and fragrance of flowers, I feel attracted to the presence of others. I have developed a centeredness within myself such that I no longer impose on others, but rather encourage them to bring forth new life within themselves by the hard work of their personal and spiritual development.

8. THE BOSSY EIGHT[1]

Where Am I as an Eight?

My Gifts

As an Eight, I have a powerful sense of justice and I bring a lot of courage to the fight for justice. I am not afraid of getting bruised in the battle of life. I also bring zest into any situation in which I am engaged. I am forceful, direct, and honest in the expression of what I hold to be the truth. I am willing to make great sacrifices in protecting my friends from being taken advantage of by others.

My Childhood

As a child I found out that it was necessary to be aggressive in order to hold my own and win the respect of others. Perhaps I had the experience of being dominated by one or both of my parents, or another authority figure, and I decided that I had to put up a strong front and never give in. Gradually I came to enjoy being a forceful person and proving my strength over opponents.

My Pride

As an Eight, I take pride in being a strong person. I look down on weakness, and take pains to present myself as a forceful personality to others. In entering any situation, I spontaneously ask who is in charge here. I need to know where the power is situated.

---

[1] Cf Beesing, et al, pp. 12f, 43-45, 90-93, 101f, 110, 119, 123, 125-128, 136, 148, 160f, 175f, 191f, 198, 209, 217f.

I see life as a warfare, and am convinced that others will take advantage of me if I am not strong. To keep up my own self-worth I need to be ready to meet head-on whatever or whoever is attacking. Being in control of any situation I am in has become essential to my feeling secure. Otherwise I feel anxious.

Time

As an Eight, I am determined not to let time dominate me. I see time as something stretching out flatly with only a few interesting features. I decide what is significant and make that the milestone for measurement. As for future time, I want to get my projects completed as rapidly as possible, even though I do not know exactly when that will be. What I want is that everything move at the pace I set. I tend to arrive early for meetings so that I do not have to attend to the clock.

Talking Style

As an Eight I tend to consider dialogue as convincing the other of the truth. I mainly want to make a statement to others. I insist that they hear me out until I have completed what I have to say on the subject. I expect that once others have understood what I have to say they will agree with me. I make my statement not only by words but also non-verbally by assertive bodily posture and dress. I say whatever pleases me, and I expect others to deal with me as I am. This is my way of relating with others.

I tend to use vulgar language. It comes right out of my gut. I do not use it to be funny or impress others, but just to emphasize my strength of personality. I feel it sounds right coming from my mouth.

Avoidance

To understand my character as an Eight, I need to see that I equate strength with goodness and see weakness as a great evil to be avoided. When asserting myself I do not let myself dwell on doubts about my own position, nor am I particularly receptive to arguments from others which contradict the stand I am taking. I can sense when others are weak and I will attack them at their weak spot, not only to defend myself, but sometimes simply because I disdain weakness in anybody.

Retaliation

As an Eight, I am a firm believer in *retaliation*. Those who are unjust are to suffer for their misdeeds. I see life as a warfare, and I have to be watchful not to be tripped up by others. Any fear or insecurity causes me to react by punishing the source of the threat. When injured or contradicted, I will redress the wrong done to me by making the other suffer in some way. In this I am the one who decides what is just. Those who contradict me are not showing me the respect I deserve as a strong person.

Intimidation

Since for me being strong preserves my own dignity, I feel good whenever I assert myself, particularly when I am contending with an opponent. I seek to control the situation by intimidating the other. I do not feel remorse in this, because I see it as good to be strong and to make others respect me.

Cantankerousness

Since I enjoy combat, I may get restless when there is nobody to confront and no challenge to face. In such cases I may begin to stir up trouble just to have a feeling of strength. Since being strong has to be felt if it is to be fulfilling for me, I enjoy a fight. By making another deal with me I feel I am relating effectively with that person. I am even ready to fight with my friends. An angry exchange between us does no seem to me to disrupt our relationship; indeed, I believe having it out with one another can strengthen our bond by clearing the air. I do not hold grudges.

I do not respect a weak opponent; my attention goes to those who have the greatest power. I often feel an inner need to pull down those who are in powerful positions. The more powerful the person is, the more likely I will be able to point out his or her weakness. I readily see through the pretenses of others, and I enjoy unmasking their hypocrisy. I tend to believe there is a need for a radical change in the authority structure in which we live, and I am inclined to take a lead in such a worthy endeavor.

Fulfillment

As an Eight I take pride mainly in how I am as a person. For that reason I find my fulfillment proving I am a strong person. I like to move out against others as a way to gain respect. It is also a defense strategy to defend my good name. I take it for granted that others will look up to me if I am forceful.

For me to be strong means to be in control. This often has a spatial dimension. I feel more secure when I extend my area of control. I do not feel remorseful about asserting myself forcefully and taking over turf from others. I think my own control gains the respect of others for me.

Preferred Center

As an Eight, I have chosen to function mainly from my gut center. I want others to deal with me, and I feel I can go with the flow of my energy whenever I interact with others. I feel most alive when in confrontation. Living out of my gut center, I have confidence in being able to react spontaneously and authentically in the engagement. Such interaction gives me a sense of my own dignity and strength. I concentrate on being present and on being myself.

I have a wing on my head center. This is experienced as being somewhat at home in thinking. I am reflective and seek to understand objectively how everything fits together. My real neglect is in the functioning of my heart center. I am not good at distinguishing various feelings and I do not care whether or not others like me. What I want is respect. In personal relationships I tend to substitute my instinctive functioning for the functioning of the heart center by relating to another by asserting myself and making that person deal with me. I do not want to show my weak underside even to those closest to me. My way of intimacy is to protect others by my strength, and to warn them to stick up for themselves, rather than take a lot of guff from some authority figure.

Where Do I Want To Go as an Eight?

Not Moving With the Arrow

As I try to understand my own character as a Eight, I may get down on myself when I discover I am domineering. Should I respond to this by withdrawing from others, I will only compound my problem. This would be to move with the arrow of compulsion toward the ego-stingy Five.

What I definitely need to avoid is to withdraw from interaction with others, and put myself into solitude to seek knowledge for its own sake. I am an activist, and I need to remain so to be healthy. I should never think that I can become a better person by becoming stingy in any way, whether with my money, time, or the gift of my presence. What I need is more interaction with others, not less. If I become solitary, I risk being selfish and sulky.

Moving Against the Arrow

The way to diffuse my aggressivity as an Eight is to move against the arrow of compulsion to the pride of the Two, who says, "I am helpful." To seek to serve the needs of a special other is just what I need as an Eight, since I tend to step on the toes of others, even of my friends, and not be in touch with my tenderness. As an Eight I really am a marshmallow inside, but I hide this from myself as well as from others.

I can get more in touch with my tender side by trying to win the affection and esteem of another through care-giving. In my intrusions into the life of my special friend, I need to adapt myself to that person's needs and simply seek to please. Through this I may make the surprising discovery that to love means to give in. Since I am so used to establishing relationships by imposing myself, to ask what I can do so that another will like me can awaken me to the world of the human heart.

From Traps to Holy Ideas

My trap as a Eight is to go around looking for a fight. I have tended to assert myself at the expense of others. Not only do I like to be against others, but also over others by being in control and getting the center of attention. This behavior stems from my idea of *justice*, which I interpret as upholding my individual rights so that I am respected. Since I do not respect weakness, I assume others will not respect me unless I prove I am strong. My strength itself becomes an assertion of right justice, and I am the one who decides what justice is. I re-structure situations and relationships to achieve my goals, and I assume others do the same for themselves.

The enneagram invites me to live out a whole different idea of justice, which is represented by the holy idea of COMPASSION. St. Paul calls compassion, or mercy, the way God makes his justice known.[2] God's standard of justice is that of compassion for the weak, whether the weakness be that of sin or of destitution. Far from disdaining the weak and respecting the strong, God bends down to human weakness and lifts it up.[3] Instead of balancing the scales of justice through retaliation, Jesus teaches us to love our enemies, to do good to those who injure us, and to be compassionate as our heavenly Father is compassionate.[4]

God's way of living out divine compassion was to have Jesus be humiliated even to death on a cross. The apostle Peter wanted to defend Jesus from being overcome by his enemies, but Jesus rebuked Peter, saying that he was

---

[2] Cf Rm 3:25f.
[3] Cf Mary's Magnificat, Lk 1:46-55.
[4] Lk 6:27-36.

93

thinking in a man's way but not in God's way.[5]   We are not to vie with our enemies by matching them strength for strength, but are to treat them with tolerance, mercy, and forgiveness.[6]   Jesus even tells us we should avoid judging the moral state of others, since God will judge us with the same standard we use on others.[7]

As an Eight, I am invited to incorporate into my life this holy idea of compassion. Since I enjoy a challenge, the enneagram invites me to grapple with myself on how to live out these New Testament teachings on compassion, and how to avoid judging my enemies. How am I to do good to enemies so as to be known as a follower of Jesus?

Jesus' way, of course, was based on the belief that anyone can be converted through our good works. For me to overcome unjust oppressors by force is not likely to lead them to discover they are acting unjustly. They do not conclude that my might makes me right. On the other hand, if they cause me harm and I do not retaliate, they will be more likely to see they are doing wrong. This, at least, is what happened in the crucifixion of Jesus, because fifty days later, at the preaching of Peter in Jerusalem at Pentecost, the Jews were struck with repentance for having allowed an innocent man to be crucified.[8]

From Passion to Virtue

Before I abandoned myself to God by embracing divine compassion as my basic stance toward others, in place of my false idea of justice and retaliation, I readily

---

[5] Mt 16:21-23.

[6] Cf Jesus' words of forgiveness on the Cross, Lk 23:34.

[7] Mt 7:1, Lk 6:37.

[8] Ac 2:37-41.

accepted in my soul the passion of *arrogance*. I did not consider that relationships with others mainly concerned tenderness and sensitivity to people's feelings. I thought I was good mainly because I could assure respect for my dignity by being a strong person before others and not showing weakness. It really meant being *boss* in any situation, being the one in control. I did not suffer remorse of conscience if I intimidated another; instead, I despised any weakness others showed. Their weakness was their problem.

Whenever I was threatened by the strength of another, my spontaneous reaction was to pull the rug out from under the other in order to gain control. When challenged by another, I certainly did not respond with a gentle disposition. If I did not punish the other, I at least made the person leave me alone, perhaps by saying: "Get off my back." I tended to choose vulgar language to show my strength and courage.

As an Eight, I was prone to give orders, but found it very hard to take orders. Here somehow the golden rule did not register with me, namely, "do unto others as you would have them do unto you."[9] Independence was almost a god to me, and so I did not let others gain control over me by giving me orders. I liked to probe and test people by my directness and forcefulness. If they could not stand the pressure, that was their problem. I really did feel good about my personal power.

To accept compassion as my spirituality represents a revolution for me on how I see others. Instead of despising their weaknesses and vices, I see myself as called to help them grow in self-esteem. I have come to see that I need others in my life in order to be a good person. Friend-

---

[9] Mt 7:12.

ship, rather than gaining respect, is really that which fills the yearnings of my heart.

What attracts me most about Jesus now is not his casting the money-changers out of the temple,[10] or his diatribe against the Scribes and Pharisees,[11] but rather his *simplicity* in the way he treated people, however they were, without probing and testing them, or in any way trying to prove he was stronger. He made himself companion with both poor and wealthy, with both men and women, with weak sinners and with those strong in faith. In the simplicity of his human friendliness, I see him practicing what he preached: we are to imitate the simplicity of little children in order to enter the Kingdom of God.[12]

Totems

In my Eightness, I was given the totem of the *rhinoceros*. I met the world with an armored personality, ready to topple over whatever got in my way, or was a threat to my security or that of my friends. Since trouble could come from any direction, my instinct was to charge first and ask questions later. I took for granted that to live well I had to be thick-skinned.

As a redeemed Eight, I have been given a new totem: the TIGER. I enjoy the native strength of my Eight personality, but I can now accept that I am just a big pussycat. I do not see I have to fight somebody or something to prove my worth. I take pride in being loyal to those with whom I live or work. Like a tiger, I know how to be playful and affectionate. My strength is camouflaged and in re-

---

[10] Mt 21:12f.

[11] Mt 23.

[12] Mt 18:3.

serve, ready if it is needed to stand up against an oppressor. I have found that nothing now causes me to be afraid, and thus, even when acting against injustice, I can preserve a gentle disposition.

9. THE LAID-BACK NINE[1]

Where Am I as a Nine?

My Gifts

As a Nine, I am a good mediator between people. I have a sense of how to show opposing sides that their differences are not that great. People find me impartial and very good at listening to them and identifying with their concerns and opinions. It is easy for me to counsel those who are troubled, for I have a natural appreciation for what is good in others and what is most important to them. People find me a friendly companion as they try to sort out their life journey.

My laid-back approach to life can help others slow down and take life easier. I see most of the hectic activity of others as getting in the way of the peacefulness we are all called to enjoy with one another and with our own self.

My Childhood

As a child, I felt neglected. Whatever I said or did really did not matter much to others. Probably I experienced little real affection from others. I came to see that complaining, and insisting that others hear me out only made matters worse. Consequently, I became resigned to blending in with others and going along with their attitudes and opinions, rather than expressing what I really thought or wanted. I sort of put myself in neutral, and occupied myself with small satisfactions or hobbies. I did not think

---

[1] Cf Beesing, et al., pp. 12f, 45-48, 94-98, 104, 109, 119, 123, 132, 140f, 148f, 168-170, 176f, 192, 198f 209f, 218.

that anything I did would be seen by others as having much importance.

Time

Time seems to slip by me whether I am doing my work or just puttering around. I like to follow a routine, whether it is work or diversion, and so the minutes and hours just tick away. When someone asks me to add something to my schedule, I do not see any way to get it done until I have completed everything already on my list. Whether I am on time or not on time does not seem of great importance as long as I keep moving, nor do I see it makes much difference whether a thing is done on time or not, just as long as it gets done.

Talking Style

As a Nine, I do not express much feeling as I talk. My non-verbal expression lacks enthusiasm and warmth. There isn't much bodily vigor to accompany the monotone in my voice. Sometimes others have a hard time hearing what I say, because my words lack emphasis and I may lower my voice at the end of a sentence. I do not really put myself forward before others. Any anger I have tends to be stuffed down, and gets expressed by my stubbornness and passive-aggressiveness.

Avoidance

What I most avoid as a Nine is *conflict*. I can't feel good about myself if I am tense. I also feel better when I am not intense. This may mean that I have to maintain my calm by withdrawing from people and situations that are hectic or brutal. I can get a lot of work done when I have a routine, but not when I am being pushed.

Indolent

As a Nine, my ego-fixation is *indolence*. This does not mean that I am afraid of hard work, but that I have *a poor sense of priorities*, and may fail to do what I am supposed to be doing because I get side-tracked by diversions. Whatever I do I tend to do in a routine way, so when I get sidetracked I just keep doing the diversion until it is too late to get my real job done. Anyway, I like to putter around and do things that do not require much attention on my part.

Lack of Energy

A major problem of mine is my *lack of energy*. Often I just cannot get myself going. Inside me there is a lot of inertia. When I do get going I keep going, but when I stop I stay stopped, and it may take a bomb to get me moving again. I just do not have much start-up ability. I look for what is outside myself for stimulation. Since I do not get excited about much of anything, I have a tendency to put things off, while making some slim excuse.

Unfocused

As a Nine I tend to be *unfocused*. My lack of priorities stems from my difficulty in deciding what I really want. I tend to merge myself with the opinions and interests of others, without really deciding for myself what I appreciate and love. Distractions readily become major pursuits of mine, such as playing cards, collecting things, or just hanging around. Since I am a laid-back person, I like to cling to what is familiar, and do not readily focus myself on one goal to the exclusion of all other goals. Often I know what I don't want much better than what I do want.

It is just hard for me to form my own opinion and set my own goals.

Fulfillment

As a Nine, I seek fulfillment by withdrawing from others in order to enhance my own personal worth. I have learned to withdraw when my environment does not offer me much in appreciation or love. I am resigned to expect little from myself or others. For me, *to be is to be content.* No matter what happens I feel I will be fulfilled as long as I am content.

To have real life, I have to be at peace. When there is conflict or intensity around me I have to withdraw to find peace, unless somehow I can induce the others to become more easy-going. Even if a life of peace may be dull, for me it does constitute the best that life has to offer. I just need to keep myself settled.

Preferred Center

As a Nine, I am a gut person. This seems a contradiction because I have so little vital energy. I live out of my gut center by living by habit and by planting myself down in a place. I often use my gut center to substitute for feeling and for thinking. As regards feeling, I keep my personal relationships on a habitual level. I like the convenience of old friends or buddies, and don't care to work at making new friends. As for thinking, I have a repetitious kind of knowing, whether it is in following the same sports' events year by year, or whether it in mulling over past experiences. I may be in a rut, but I enjoy not having to gear up for something new. I do not react spontaneously with a lot of feeling when something new happens.

Where Do I Want To Go as a Nine?

Not Moving With the Arrow

To discover a lot of negative things about myself through the enneagram could result in depression for some other personalities, but as a Nine I am used to thinking of myself as of little worth. I will compound my compulsion, however, if I move with the arrow to the ego-coward Six. I think I am aware instinctively of the pitfall of becoming like a Six, but, of course, it could happen. It would mean that I become apprehensive about all the demands made on me. That could drive me into despair, for I would begin to say that I am no good unless I am responsible for all sorts of demands made on me by others.

Moving Against the Arrow

My liberation as a Nine lies in moving against the arrow of compulsion to take on the pride of the Three, who says, "I am successful." My way to greater health as a Nine lies in becoming a much more enterprising person. I know I can get things done once I get going. The problem is mainly in my attitude. As a Nine, I am called to leave behind my characteristic pride in being easy-going, and replace it with the pride of being efficient. I do have it within myself to be an efficient person. By setting some goals I can focus myself so as to be able to recognize success when it occurs. My success can be measured in little steps just as well as in great attainments, but unless I accomplish something, I won't have much motive for self-esteem.

For me to imitate the personality of the Three will involve setting aside the old idea I had of not liking the world as it is. That idea led me into becoming a non-conformist. Threes, however, adjust themselves to the world in order to make a good impression. They sell themselves in order to sell their product. Can I do that as a Nine? How about making myself more attractive in how I dress and how I express myself? Could I cultivate more interests so as to be more interesting to others? Maybe I need to ask myself the basic questions of why am I here on earth and what am I called to do.

From Traps to Holy Ideas

Once I have recognized I have the problems typical of the Nine, I need to see that I will never find a real liberation unless I turn to God with all my heart. The good news of salvation is especially addressed to me as a Nine because it concerns God's love. If I did not experience as a child that others loved me for being who I am, then it has always been difficult for me to entertain the message of God's love for me. I have simply been trapped in the idea *self-abasement*. As such I have a desperate need to accept the holy idea of UNCONDITIONAL LOVE.

God's love, of course, is always a free gift, but our ideas of ourselves, of others, and of God can block our accepting this love God has for us. This was the case with the opponents of Jesus during his public ministry. To know Jesus' message of unconditional love, I need to identify myself with him as a recipient of the Father's love. As is said in John 17:26, God loves both Jesus and me with the same love.

For me as a Nine, abandonment to God means the discovery of the reality of God's unconditional love for me. This needs to be more than a belief; it must become a principle of life. Often Christian teachings are held more in the head than in the heart, and what people today say they believe they do not really believe. For me as a Nine, however,

I need to depend on Jesus' message of God's unconditional love in order to be happy in this world. I cannot find my own humanity without it. Most likely such love was denied me as I grew up, and so I am one of the lowly persons whom God wishes to lift up through Christ's coming.[2]

Unconditional Love becomes real for me when I see myself as truly lovable simply because of who I am. That thought may bring tears to my eyes. I have craved to be so loved! Now it is offered to me by God's grace. By assenting to the holy idea of unconditional love, I do not so much believe in God, as I believe that God believes in me. My Creator has made me as a unique gift to the world at this time in history. I cannot be that gift from God to others, however, if I continue to cling to my old idea of self-abasement. I must stop x-ing myself out, because God cannot give a negative gift. After all, God made me, and God does not make junk.

From Passion to Virtue

To no one as much as to me as a Nine is the truth so applicable that unless I first love myself I cannot love others. Admiration and affection for others is made possible only by first having admiration and affection for myself. It is like using a computer: what we put in is what we get out. If the input is garbage, the output will be garbage. If, however, I put into myself a belief in my own lovableness, the output of my actions will tend to express to others my belief in their lovableness as well.

By loving me, God loves into me certain gifts and talents. As a consequence of my abandonment to unconditional love, I am led to discern the unique gifts and talents I

---

[2] Cf Lk 1:52.

have. To recognize these gifts and talents, I will need the help of others. Especially I need someone with a loving heart to mirror back to me what is within me. I may find that once I start loving myself unconditionally, I will notice others knocking on my heart with such love for me. Perhaps I did not recognize this before, either because I could not believe I was lovable, or because I did not value sufficiently the importance of being loved.

The discovery of God's sending persons to me to love me with Jesus' own love can awaken in me a whole new interest in life itself. This may unlock within me a new, intense yearning to develop myself, so as to make my gifts more available to others. I will see myself not simply as a peacemaker, or an advocate of taking life easy, but much more I will sense myself on mission to better the lives of others in some professional way. Having become aware of the power of growth within myself, I will want to enkindle in others a yearning to grow. As Jesus said, the Kingdom of God is within us.[3] We need to let it come by believing in our own personal and spiritual growth.

Totems

As a compulsed Nine, I was like an *elephant*. I had big ears, but often did not listen to what was being said. I did not understand how others had to accommodate themselves to the weight of my own presence, even should I only be taking a snooze after work. Often others had a hard time getting me to move on to some other place, or even to move at all.

Now as a redeemed Nine, I have been given the new totem of the PORPOISE. I am much more friendly and

---

[3] Lk 17:21.

willing to cooperate with others. I see that the peace I want to bring to the lives of others can only be brought about if we work together to create a civilization of love, beginning with our own community of friends. I can relax with others much better now, because I know my own great worth as a person and how others appreciate who I am. Because I see myself as a unique gift to others, I have become more outgoing with my feelings. I know there will never be another person with exactly the same gifts that I have. I am placed here to share my gifts with others for their own betterment, and to draw us together into shared life.

B.
Enneagram Spirituality

10. JUNGIAN THEORY AND THE ENNEAGRAM

Hopefully, the foregoing résumés of the nine enneagram types have whetted the appetite to study the inner dynamics of the enneagram system. As a preliminary to this study, it can be helpful to reflect on some similarities of the enneagram theory with Jungian theory. Participants in my workshops usually arrive with considerable knowledge of the Jungian theory, certainly much more than they know about the enneagram. In particular most of them have already sought to know themselves through the Myers-Briggs Type Indicator. They want to know how the enneagram coincides with what they already know about themselves through that typology. If the reader is not already familiar with his or her personality as described by Jungian theory, it may be best simply to skip reading this chapter, since the rest of the book in no way depends on what I write here. This chapter's purpose is to move from what is better known, namely, Jungianism, to what is less known, namely, the enneagram.

For those already knowledgeable of Jungian personality theory, I like to point out four entry points into the enneagram system from Carl Jung's insights:

- Developmental Typologies

- The Functions

- The Shadow

- The Differentiation of Personality Types.

Developmental Typologies

Both the Jungian system and the enneagram are developmental typologies. Their very purpose in describing one's particular personality type is to indicate a point of departure for personal growth, especially in the second half of life. I was probably between the ages of four and six years old when I began to form my ego, and thereby began both the actualization and limitation of what I wanted to become as a person. Because of my need to develop the ego for survival and self-identity, there have been certain "roads not taken" in the realization of my human personality, and as a mature adult I need to grapple with them. By ascertaining my personality type through either Jungianism or through the enneagram, I am given a particular method to get in touch with potentialities I earlier overlooked or suppressed.

The crisis of middle age is precisely the need and challenge to see more in life than I counted on in my youth. Either typology provides me with a direction to take to actualize what has been unactualized, and to overcome the imbalance and bias of my human personality. To understand such imbalance and lost potential, I need to know the basic functions of personality, and to find out which of my functions is underdeveloped, so I know what I need to develop in myself to attain greater *wholeness.*

The Functions

The dynamics of personality in both the Jungian system and the enneagram system are rooted in a set of *functions* of the psyche. The Jungian system has four functions:

(F) feeling—(N) intuition—(T) thinking—(S) sensation.

112

The enneagram has only three functions:

(HEART) feeling—(HEAD) thinking—(GUT) instinct.

The dynamic inherent in Jungian theory of functions is that of sets of opposites: *feeling—thinking,* and *intuition—sensation.* Since the enneagram has only three functions, they cannot be adequately opposed to one another.

Because of this difference in the basic dynamics of the personality,—with four Jungian functions and three enneagram functions,—comparing Jungian theory with the enneagram always will be like comparing apples and oranges. These two theories will never completely coincide, but they can complement one another in helping me to know myself and to develop my potential.

Certain similarities in nomenclature used in both systems could deceive me into assuming that like terms have like meaning. I need to recognize that the function of *Jungian feeling* differs from that of *enneagram feeling,* and *Jungian thinking* differs from *enneagram thinking.* In the **Jungian system**, feeling and thinking can be described as follows:

Through *feeling* I make judgments based on my *subjective* values.

Through *thinking* I make judgments based on *objective* facts and principles.

In the **enneagram system**, feeling and thinking are described quite differently:

Through *feeling* I am concerned about *relating* and interacting.

113

Through *thinking* I am concerned about knowing *how to fit in.*

Dominant and Secondary Functions

Among the four functions in the Jungian theory each personality type has a *dominant function* and a *secondary function*. There is also a third function which also is somewhat available to me, but the fourth and last function is deeply shrouded in the unconscious and therefore rather undifferentiated. This makes this hidden fourth function threatening to me both within my inner world and when I meet it in the personality of another. It contains trapped and unconscious personal energy. Jungian theory has various strategies for uncovering and rendering available to the consciousness some of the energy trapped in the unconscious.

The enneagram theory of three functions resonates with these Jungian insights. In the enneagram the self is described as unbalanced because instead of my using all three of my functions in action appropriate to each, I have chosen one of the three as my preferred way of functioning as a person. It constitutes my dominant function, or "preferred center." Although the question of a secondary function is more complex than in Jungianism, it does exist in the enneagram system. I theorize about it in the way I describe "wings."[1] The third and last function in the enneagram is somewhat like the Jungian fourth function. This third enneagram function tends to be undifferentiated and not put to use in the personality. It constitutes a challenge for me to recover its use. In most cases recovering its use

---

[1] Cf Chapter 12, where I take up in detail the three enneagram functions, or "centers."

can give me much more balance and move me into a re-markable change in personality through my taking on the pride of the opposing type, a process called "moving against the arrow of compulsion."[2]

Complementarity of Functions

Since the functions of each system denote different operations of the personality according to distinct needs and situations, by nature the different functions are complementary to one another. This is particularly obvious in the Jungian system, where persons who have different dominant functions are needed for the smooth operation of a management team. This is often demonstrated in management training through what is called the POWER CYCLE.

The power cycle designates a planning process which moves from *EVALUATION* to *RECOMMENDATION* to *DECISION* to *ACTION*, and then repeats the cycle by continuing with EVALUATION. The four Jungian functions correspond to these four steps in the planning process, and so a management team needs to have members of all four dominant types to carry out well the planning process. *Feelers* are natural evaluators; *intuitives* are recommenders; *thinkers* are adept in making decisions; *sensates* are good at action.

Should it happen that a team has many more *intuitives* than *sensates*, there may be great enthusiasm to plan, but much less energy to carry out the plans in action. Intuitives always have many ideas for recommendations on what to do, but much less inclination to get down to the nuts and bolts of action. Similarly, many who are given administra-

---

[2] Cf Chapter 13, where I consider moving against the instinct of compulsion as part of "instinctual conversion."

The Power Cycle

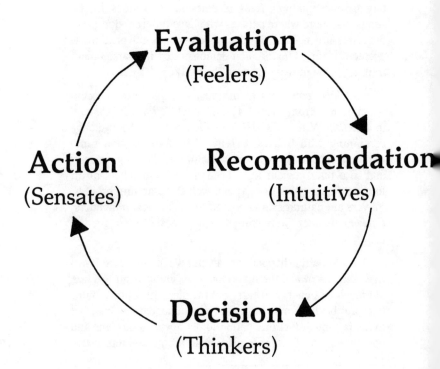

Evaluation
(Feelers)

Action
(Sensates)

Recommendation
(Intuitives)

Decision
(Thinkers)

tive positions may tend to be *thinkers* and therefore be adept in making decisions, but where do they find the *feelers* to evaluate the needs and desires of clients?

When a management team does have persons with all four types as dominant functions, there is a built-in problem in the exercise of the process, because the very complementarity of functioning can also cause antipathy between persons of opposing dominant types. *Feelers* and *thinkers*, being opposites, tend to threaten one another, as is also the case between *intuitives* and *sensates*.

When the team begins with EVALUATION, the *feelers* are at home in sharing how clients are feeling, but as the *feelers* go on and on evaluating, the *thinkers* may become impatient to get down to making a decision, which they probably have clearly in mind already. *Thinkers* tend to view a meeting on evaluation as largely a distraction from the business at hand, and thus a waste of precious time.

When the time comes to make RECOMMEN-DATIONS, the *intuitives* will have a field day, but while they are sharing their ideas of what could be done, the *sensates* may find this very threatening and even reckless. The security of *sensates* rests on the tried and proven, and what is as yet untried, and hence unproven, will cause them anxiety.

When the *thinkers* are given the opportunity to make a DECISION, their opposites, the *feelers*, will feel anxious because they will fear someone will not like the decision or may even be hurt by it. The *thinkers* simply look at a problem objectively and rationally, and having made the decision they will be mostly concerned with reasons for the decision, rather than with how others will feel about it.

When the *sensates* finally get their turn by getting into the ACTION of carrying out the decision, the *intuitives* probably will not be on the scene to help with the work.

In the *enneagram system*, the complementarity of different personality types is an area of very worthwhile study in human relationships. Undoubtedly a community or team made up of different types will have a richness of perspective and superior capabilities of action, provided that their differences as persons are accepted and appreciated rather than resented. We have a certain built-in antipathy toward that which contradicts the pride of our type. Nines may dislike Sixes because the latter are so rigid, Ones may dislike Fours for being so hypersensitive, Twos may dislike Eights for being so uncaring, and so on.

The Shadow

Another area of similarity between Jungianism and the enneagram concerns the Jungian *shadow*. The shadow reminds us of Mr. Hyde in Robert Lewis Stephenson's tale, *Dr. Jekyll and Mr. Hyde*. When my ego strives to function according to high ideals, that very idealism is like a bright light casting a shadow within the psyche. The brighter the light, i.e., the greater the idealism I strive to live, the darker will be the shadow. This shadow refers to what is hidden to my consciousness because it contradicts and thwarts the high motives I have accepted for myself. Do-gooders such as Dr. Jekyll may have a very vicious shadow self which undermines their high idealism. They may even act it out in a shadowy way, such that they live an unacknowledged "double life" of both virtue and its opposite vice.

Because in actuality the shadow undermines our idealistic motives as we go about doing good for others, Jungians have sought to give warnings about the shadow to those in the helping professions, such as physicians, counselors, social workers, and the clergy.[3] All of us who have high ideals of service are likely to be unconsciously motivated to use others for our advantage, while all the time professing to be serving them for their benefit.

The enneagram can be seen as a remarkable tool to investigate and grapple with the Jungian shadow. This is because the enneagram deals mainly with motivation, and the vicious side of the shadow has a lot to do with hidden motives. We could say that the main benefit of the enneagram is the light it throws on our shadow, and the guidance it gives us for overcoming the shadow's destructive power.

The Differentiation of Personality Types.

Jungian personality theory employs various pairs of opposites to differentiate sixteen personality types. To illustrate this, let us use the formula of four letters from the Myers-Briggs Type Indicator. We will take the formula INFJ by way of example.

Introvert/Extrovert

The *first letter* of the formula INFJ indicates that this personality type is (I) introvert rather than (E) extrovert. For Carl Jung, the distinction of introvert/extrovert is the most important factor in discovering our personality. Introverts and extroverts can function very well both pri-

---

[3] Cf Adolf Guggenbühl-Craig, *Power in the Helping Professions,* Spring Publication, Inc., Dallas, Texas, 1971.

vately and publicly; their difference lies in what energizes them, and what drains them.

For introverts interaction with others will be a drain of energy. They need solitude to recover their energy. Extroverts, on the other hand, acquire energy by interacting with others. For them, solitude is a drain of energy. By being with others they acquire the energy needed to be alone. At a gathering of people where there is a lot of healthy interaction, extroverts will generally become more and more stimulated by talking, while introverts will tend to tire the longer the conversation goes on.

In the second half of life, which begins at middle age, our psyche senses a need to recover what has been lost or undeveloped. One's personal task then as an extrovert is to become more introverted, and as an introvert to become more extroverted. In our American culture, which is heavily extroverted in contrast with some introverted oriental cultures, introverts often feel inferior and left out in the first half of life, but in the second half of life they find our culture of great assistance as they grow more able to be energized by social life. Extroverts, on the other hand, are favored in our society in the first half of life, but in the second half of life they have a hard struggle in becoming more introverted. Consequently, as Jung remarked, there is a balance of justice: in the first half of life extroverts tend to be happier and more content with themselves, whereas introverts are apt to get along better and be more satisfied with themselves in the second half of life. After the age of fifty, these differences tend to even out, as extroverts discover they are energized also by being alone, and introverts grow accustomed to be energized also by the stimulus of interaction with others. Despite these recoveries of energy, however, our type does not change. According to the theory, we always remain basically either an introvert or an extrovert.

In the *enneagram* there is no designation of persons as introvert or extrovert. It is difficult, however, to imagine the 7 or 8 as introverted, and just as difficult to imagine the 5 or 6 as extroverted. The aggressive types (8, 1, 3) are usually extroverts, and to them we need to add the 7 and the 2. The withdrawing types (5, 9, 4) are usually introverts, and to these we should add the 6. Although that designates five types (8, 1, 2, 3, 7) as extroverted and only four types (5, 6, 9, 4) as introverted, the 3 may sometimes be introverted, and other types may also deviate from what seems to be the norm.

Perception

The *second letter* of the Myers-Briggs' formula is that of the perceptive functions, either N (intuitive) or S (sensate). The N, or intuitive function, perceives the big picture, such as "the forest," and the S, or sensate function, perceives detail, such as "the trees." Intuition is at home in the unknown future; sensation is at home in the past, the tried and proven. Intuitives are bored or frustrated by following past traditions; sensates are threatened by change. Intuitives find their security in trying out what is new; sensates feel secure and content with repeating the past.

In the *enneagram* there is no corresponding function indicating either intuition or sensation. For this reason, those who have discovered their enneagram type can benefit a great deal by knowing also their Myers-Briggs classification, since recognizing intuition and sensation is very helpful in understanding one's giftedness, and also in knowing one's direction of growth. Intuitives need to avoid more futuring than they can realize in action, and sensates need to open themselves to a broader vision, which may come to them through others who are more intuitive.

Judgment

The *third letter* of the Myers-Briggs' formula represents the judgmental functions, either F (feeling) or T (thinking). *Feelers* judge by personal values and ideals; *thinkers* judge by facts and principles. It is to be noted that in the enneagram the heart center, which is the feeling function, is not a judgmental function. It stands for the ability to relate favorably with others, and for considering relationships as very important in life. The Jungian feeling function and the enneagram feeling function are similar, however, in that they both convey warmth of feeling and consider feelings as very important. That the Jungian feeling function and the enneagram feeling function do not coincide becomes evident once many persons know both their enneagram type and their Myers-Briggs formula. Persons whose dominant is feeling on the Myers-Briggs may not be heart persons (2, 3, 4) on the enneagram.

This lack of correlation is also true regarding the Jungian thinking function and the enneagram thinking function. Enneagram thinking is not one mainly of judgment based on facts and principles. As stated earlier, its concern is how one fits into the environment.

Dominant/Secondary

The *fourth letter* of the Myers-Briggs' formula is J (judgmental) or P (perceptive). It is an indicator of how one deals with the outside world. It is not a separate function, though it is often misunderstood as such. Because many assume it designates another function, they talk about being a "heavy J" or a "heavy P," and overlook the key role of the fourth letter in pointing out their dominant function. Many end up knowing their four-lettered formula, but not knowing their dominant function. This may not bother some people, but it does suggest that they have moved too far away from the Jungian system to benefit from it as a developmental typology. After all, the dominant is decisive in knowing the greatest giftedness of our personality type, and in pointing out which functions are underdeveloped.

How, then, does the fourth letter of the Myers-Briggs' formula indicate the dominant function?

In the formula INFJ, the J indicates that I deal with the outside world with the judgmental function indicated by the *third letter*. In this case, the third letter is F (feeling). It could have been T (thinking) as the alternative judgmental function. Should the fourth letter have been P, instead of J, it would have pointed to the *second letter* as the perceptive function I use to deal with the outside world. In this case of INFJ, that function is N (intuition), though it could have been S (sensation) as the alternative perceptive function.

This still does not tell me my dominant function because of the difference in the attitude of extroverts and introverts. Extroverts, of course, use their dominant function to deal with the outside world, but introverts use their dominant function to deal with their *inside world*. Consequently, when the P or J points out how the personality deals with the outside world, this will be the dominant function in the extrovert (E), but only the *secondary function* in the introvert (I). In the latter case, the other middle letter will be the dominant.

In the final step for determining my dominant function, I look at the first letter of the formula (I or E). If I am an introvert (I), then the P or J will point to my *secondary function,* and I will see that the other middle letter constitutes my dominant. From our initial example, INFJ, the J points to the third letter, F, as the function used for dealing with the outside world. Since the personality is introverted (I), the function dealing with the outside world, *feeling* (F), will be the secondary function. The dominant will be the second letter, N, designating *intuition*, since as an introvert I focus primarily on my inside world. As an INFJ I am an introverted, feeling *intuitive.* It is very important to know that my personality is intuitive as well as introverted.

Should I be ENFJ, the J designates that I deal with the outside world by the third letter, which is F. Since as an extrovert (E) I deal with the outside world with my dominant function, that third letter (F) is my dominant function. As an ENFJ I am an extroverted, intuitive *feeler.* Very readily as INFJ, a person could be a Five on the enneagram, but never as ENFJ. As an ENFJ, a person might be a One, but never as INFJ. Such examples show there is some relation between Jungian types and enneagram types, even though they do not truly correlate.

From the factors we have discussed in the Myers-Briggs' formula, each of the four Jungian functions (N, S, F, T) can have four variations as dominants: for example, dominant N may be I or E, and have as secondary function either F or T. The result is a system of sixteen distinct personalities: INFJ, ENFJ, INFP, ENFP, ISFJ, ESFJ, ISFP, ESFP, INTJ, ENTJ, INTP, ENTP, ISTJ, ESTJ, ISTP, ESTP.

Needless to say, this makes Jungian typology more complex than the enneagram typology of only nine types, numbered 1 to 9. On the other hand, if one omits consideration of the secondary function in the Jungian typology, there are only eight types, which approximates the number of nine in the enneagram. These eight Jungian types are described as follows:

- extroverted and introverted *feelers*

- extroverted and introverted *intuitives*

- extroverted and introverted *thinkers*

- extroverted and introverted *sensates*

Even if people are satisfied with distinguishing personality by only eight basic Jungian types, I still believe the enneagram of nine types is easier to understand and to use as a guide for self-improvement. It is my experience that the enneagram system indicates more clearly, and surely more simply, *where I am* and *where I need to go*. The enneagram will seem less *rational*, however, and more like a dogma to be taken on faith. It is offered as wisdom from an oral tradition. Whether or not it is true wisdom leading to wholeness and greater happiness is to be proven by trying it on "for size." Once I identify with a given type, I am invited to acknowledge my compulsion and work to overcome it. "The proof (of the recipe) is in the pudding." If it is helps me to stretch myself as a person and to feel more *whole*, it has served its purpose.

Obsession/Compulsion

This leads to the question of how Jungianism depicts what enneagram theory calls "compulsion." One answer is that the exact opposite of my Jungian dominant will be that which is deepest in the unconscious and most obsessive to me. In the case of the INFJ, for example, the obsessive type is ES, extroverted sensation. Introverted intuitives will tend to be obsessed by some minute, exterior detail. They need to know that some external detail, like turning out the lights or a typographical error in a letter, could lead to irascible conduct with an associate who is blamed for the oversight.

I have always found this explanation from Jungian theory very subtle, and even when recognizing my typical obsession, I am mystified about how to overcome it. I find the enneagram much more helpful in indicating both the obsession and the remedy. The Jungian system remains highly sophisticated in both its analysis and recommendations for personal development, whereas the enneagram zeros in directly on the problem of disguised motivations in my shadow, and highlights immediately the undifferentiated function which causes obsessiveness. On the other hand, such clarity in the enneagram about my "problem" can be very threatening because I may want to hide from the real truth about myself. In the enneagram I begin not by trying to know my strengths, as is the tendency in Jungian theory, but by uncovering my hidden *sin*.[4]

---

[4] Cf Beesing, et al., p.6: "The compulsion is a kind of 'hidden sin,' where sin is understood as a kind of paralysis or hindrance in becoming one's true authentic self."

11. DIFFERENTIATION OF THE NINE TYPES[1]

The enneagram system demonstrates that human personality evolves from the quest for personal fulfillment. Just as I am born with an physical orientation and power to grow to a certain physical completeness, so, too, in my psyche there is an orientation and power to grow to a certain *personal* completeness. Being a person involves a project of development. That project is energized by an innate longing to become fully a human person. Personal fulfillment is the attainment of a completeness of human essence, the realization of all that I am actually and potentially as human.

In the enneagram system, true fulfillment involves union. This is union with oneself, of course, such as Jungianism calls "individuation," but also union with others, with God, and with all exterior reality. I came into this world with an implicit trust that an all-embracing union with exterior reality would serve my deepest yearnings and my fondest desires. I assumed that all that surrounded me, including all persons, things, and powers, would be beneficent to me. Between the age of four and six years, however, I discovered that this was not true. Those around me contradicted my wants. I decided I could not count on a union with my social environment to fulfill my deepest desires.

This losing of trust in external reality was a "fall from society." It was great loss for me, something like the discovery by Adam and Eve that they were naked. In my need "to cover up" for defense from an alien social reality, I

---

[1] Cf Beesing, et al., pp. 99-114.

developed the *ego-consciousness* of being *separate from the world.*

By means of this ego-consciousness, I set up a defense strategy to enable me to create my own life, without being interdependent with external reality for my fulfillment. The defense strategy was to protect my ego and my worth as a person in confrontation with a world I did not wholly trust. It involved specifying who I was as a person, and what constituted my fulfillment. This was to enable me to attain fulfillment on my own, the kind of fulfillment I chose for myself.

The Self-concept

My defense strategy in separating myself from the world was crystallized through the choice of a *self-concept.* By this self-concept, I limited my awareness of who I was and of what constituted my fulfillment. It was a certain stance in relationship to the outside world, a stance of ego vs. world.

There were three possible self-concepts in relationship with the world. I chose my own self-concept from one of the following:

- "I am bigger than the world."

- "I am smaller than the world."

- "I must adjust to the world."

If my decision was that "*I am bigger than the world,*" I centered my personal fulfillment on how I was as a person. Here fulfillment was seen in terms of *self-aggrandizement*, the making of myself greater. I limited my absolute good simply to the filling up of my own person.

Any experience would be evaluated in terms of whether or not it made me more in my own being.

Through this self-concept of being bigger than the world, I chose reality to be "the inner order." I decided that reality,—or what life is really about—is the inner order, i.e., what is inside me. For me to stand out as a person, or simply "to be," what counted was my personal development, my self-actualization. As a result of this self-concept of being bigger than the world, I assumed that to experience real life I had to be an INDEPENDENT person. This was my stance if I am an EIGHT, TWO, or FIVE.

If, however, I decided that "*I am smaller than the world*," I centered my personal fulfillment on what I do to the world. To be fulfilled, I had to have a certain kind of environment, and it depended on me to create this. My experience would be evaluated by the kind of impression I made on the world, so that it would be the way I needed it to be. I chose reality to be "the outer order." For me to stand out as a person, or simply to be, I had to transform my environment according to my own image. Because of this self-concept of being smaller than the world, I assumed that to experience real life I had to be a STUBBORN person. This was my stance if I am a ONE, SEVEN, or FOUR.

If, finally, I took as my self-concept that "*I must adjust to the world*," I centered my self-fulfillment on conforming myself to the world as it is. I chose reality to be "the outer-inner harmony." For me, real life was an integration between what was inside and outside of me. This is what is called "conformity."

Although this conforming of myself to the world would be right and just in an ideal world without sin or other evils, such integration with an alienating world limited my human ideals. It meant that I was resigned to the world as it is. My self-fulfillment would consist in adjusting myself to live in harmony with the world according to its standards and demands. I would evaluate my worth in terms of how well I had achieved a harmony with the world as it is. Since I had already experienced outer reality as alien to my deepest yearnings, I was seeking my fulfillment within the ambiguous circumstances of a world I did not wholly trust. This would make me noticeably SELF-ABSORBED as a person. Such was my stance if I am a THREE, SIX, or NINE.

Mode of Behavior

My stance of ego vs. world not only involved one of these three basic ways of looking at myself called the self-concept. In order to be fulfilled though my own efforts, I chose a certain way of behavior, and this, too, was in relation to the world. This was a choice from the following three modes of behavior:[2]

- aggressive behavior (against the world)

- compliant behavior (towards the world)

- detached behavior (away from the world)

It is out of this intersection of the three self-concepts with the three modes of behavior that there arises the differentiation of the nine enneagram types. Within each of the three self-concepts there arises three distinct types.

---

[2] Credit for this distinction of three modes of behavior is given to Karen Horney, an associate of Sigmund Freud. Cf *Experiencing the Enneagram,* Andreas Ebert and Marian Küstenmacher, eds., Crossroad, New York, 1992, p. 49.

There are three independent types, three stubborn types, and three self-absorbed types, as follows:

> **INDEPENDENT**: EIGHT (aggressive)—TWO (compliant)—FIVE (detached)
>
> **STUBBORN**: ONE (aggressive)—SEVEN (compliant)—FOUR (detached)
>
> **SELF-ABSORBED**: THREE (aggressive)—SIX (compliant)—NINE (detached)

Ego-fixation

This combination of the self-concept with a mode of behavior causes a *bias* in the way I act to control my relationships. This bias is *compulsive,* because it contains within itself a patterned *drive* for the completion of myself as a person according to my chosen self-concept. The bias is called an *ego-fixation,* because my ego-consciousness of being separated from the world has been fixed, or patterned, by a certain mode of behavior for self-fulfillment.

Each of the resulting nine personality types is called a specific ego-fixation. These ego-fixations are (1) ego-resentment, (2) ego-flattery, (3) ego-vanity, (4) ego-melancholy, (5) ego-stinginess, (6) ego-cowardice, (7) ego-planning, (8) ego-vengeance, and (9) ego-indolence.[3]

Compulsion/Avoidance

By ego-fixation I get caught in a pattern of behavior that is compulsive. A *compulsion* is *a basic driving force which tends to prevail in personal behavior*. It tends to be an irresistible force from the fact that it is hidden and

---

[3] Beesing, et al., p. 135.

unrecognized.[4]   Its hidden power consists in a specific strategy to avoid something. I tend to take pride in the *avoidance* specific to my personality type, because I think that by avoiding this I am superior to others.

The specific avoidances are: (1) anger, (2) need, (3) failure, (4) ordinariness, (5) emptiness, (6) deviance, (7) pain, (8) weakness, and (9) conflict.

Pride

In ordinary parlance, the word "pride" has both positive and negative connotations. On the positive side, it designates justifiable self-respect or elation about something that deserves praise. On the negative side, it is related to such terms as "conceit," "arrogance," "disdain," and "haughtiness."

In the enneagram system, "pride" is used in both positive and negative senses. Each personality type is designated by a specific pride, as (a) *the attitude of what is most important in being a person*, and (b) *that which makes one superior to others*. The former,—that which is most important in being a person,—is inclusive of others, but the latter,—that which makes one superior to others,—is exclusive of others.

By taking on the pride specific to my personality type, I have decided that my fulfillment is to be attained by a split away from outside reality, rather than communion with it. In some way, by my pride I am saying to others, *I am worthwhile, and being worthwhile I do not need you.* I may also be saying, *I am using you, opposing you, or stepping over you in order to be worthwhile as a person.*

---

[4] Ibid., p. 5f.

The Passions[5]

Each enneagram type has a specific *passion*. I like to explain the origin of the enneagram passions through the philosophical stance that my being is programmed for fulfillment in the sense that I am vitalized with a passionate energy of love which longs for my essential completeness as a person. In other words, springing from my essence itself is a longing for fulfillment. This longing for fulfillment is my most fundamental energy as a person. Passionate love is a radical responsiveness to what is viewed as my absolute good, i.e., that for which I will sacrifice everything, because to participate in this good gives me ultimate fulfillment. Should my absolute good coincide with the name of God, then my passionate love may be called my *longing for God.*

When what I choose as my absolute good is something less than the complete realization of my human essence, I develop a *passion* specific to my personality type. I make being a person the specific "project" of my life. I define being a person by some limitation of my human essence. By this, I look at a limited good as though it were the absolute fulfillment of my person.

As a result, my responsive energy of passionate love is *distorted*, because I seek as an absolute good that which in reality is only a limited good for me. Since the limited good is made out to be my unlimited good, this false sense of reality sets up in me a *craving*. I crave to find absolute satisfaction in what can be, at most, the attainment of a series of limited goals. Instead of the term *craving*, however, the enneagram system uses the word *passion*. My passionate love for fulfillment, as distorted by a false sense of reality, creates the dominant disposition called passion.

---

[5] Cf.Beesing, et al., pp. 104f, 124f.

There is a passion specific to each personality type, namely: (1) anger, (2) pride, (3) deceit, (4) envy, (5) stinginess, (6) fear, (7) over-indulgence, (8) arrogance, (9) laziness.

The source of the enneagram passions is in itself healthy and salutary. My passion does not spring from a source that is corrupted. It does not spring from some interior poison. It is simply a *distortion* in my fundamental energy of responsive love. The passionate love is good, but it is distorted in its expression by reason of being focused on what is only in reality a limited good, instead of an absolute good. I made a mistake in how I see reality. Something is being made my fulfillment which is too limiting to human essence. The distortion arises due to my false sense of what life is about. It is a mistake that can be corrected, but only when I place my heart on what will truly complete my wholeness.

With the foregoing in mind, we are now ready to see much more in detail how the differentiation of the nine enneagram types emerges from ego-consciousness. We will begin with the self-concept of being bigger than the world.

"I am bigger than the world"

If I decide through my ego-consciousness that my fulfillment consists in being bigger than the world, I concentrate on the development of my own inner being. My personality takes a stance before others of being INDEPENDENT. In my strategy to become more, I may become an aggressive Eight, a compliant Two, or a detached Five.

EIGHT: Aggressive and Independent

As an Eight, my ego-fixation is *vengeance.* Already as a child, I decided that my personal worth could be protected and enhanced by bringing suffering to anyone who intimidated or contradicted me. As a response to the experience of outside reality trying to lord over me, I was determined to defend my personal dignity by aggressive behavior. With my self-concept of being bigger than the world, I viewed my self-fulfillment as realizable by being a strong person in confrontation with others. My strength would be consolidated by being in control of situations, and being the center of attention as the one in command.

Consequently, my specific pride as an Eight is to say, "I am powerful." For me, *to be is to be strong.* I take for granted that to be good as a person I must be strong, and that it is bad to be weak. I tend to despise any weakness in myself or others, whereas *strength* in myself and others commands my respect. For this reason, *weakness* is my specific avoidance. As an Eight, I am vigilant not to be taken advantage of in any way, lest I lose my personal dignity. I also focus on the weakness of another as an evil I am ready to attack.

My passion as an Eight is *arrogance.* This is an aggressive attitude seeking to intimidate others. Arrogance is my defensive strategy to protect my pride of being a strong person. By being arrogant and blatantly seeking to intimidate another, I experience a sense of personal aggrandizement. It feels good to me to be strong in confrontation. Since I view life as a power struggle, I see the possession of turf as very important. To express my strength, I will tend to take over the turf of another, without having any feelings of remorse. I consider such overbearing behavior as self-fulfilling, since it fosters my control of the situation, and thereby adds to my security. Above all, I see it as a way of getting *respect*.

TWO: Compliant and Independent

The second enneagram point choosing self-fulfillment in the inner order is the Two. As a Two, I am a *compliant type,* because I move toward the world for my fulfillment. My ego-fixation is *flattery,* which is acting so as to gratify and please others to win approval from them. As a Two, I decided that appreciation and approval from another constitutes my self-fulfillment. With my chosen self-concept of being bigger than the world, I see my fulfillment in being the kind of person who wins appreciation from another by complying to that other's needs. For that reason, I take pride in being a *helpful person.*

For me as a Two, *to be is to be needed.* If I am not needed by a significant other, I see myself as not a worthwhile person. At the same time, I avoid being in *need,* since I want to be in control. Just as Eights seek independence and self-sufficiency by avoiding to acknowledge any weakness, as a Two I seek independence and self-sufficiency by avoiding to acknowledge any need which would make me beholden to another.

As a Two, I make myself charming and flattering to another as a way of establishing my self-worth, and sensing my superior goodness. Similarly, just as Eights attack the *weakness* of another as an opportunity to demonstrate their own superior *strength* and control, so, as a Two, I serve the *need* I see in another as an opportunity to demonstrate that I am a very *helpful* person.

My specific passion as a Two is *pride.* My pride contradicts humility, which is the virtue acknowledging my need of others. By pride I value being self-sufficient and independent of others. If I were humble I would say, "I have need of you and your gift." Because of pride, however, I deny I have needs. Through my independent behavior I am saying, "I do not need you."

FIVE: Detached and Independent

The third independent type is the Five. Like Eights and Twos, as a Five I see my fulfillment as consisting in my own personal enhancement. My preferred behavior is withdrawal, to be *detached* from the world as the way to reach fulfillment. My ego-fixation is *stinginess,* whereby I store up my resources, rather than share them or give them to others. By being stingy with what I have and refraining from taking on commitments, I seek to preserve my independence so that I can pursue my fulfillment in my own private way.

I see my fulfillment as my being bigger than the world because of what I know. My way of controlling reality is to know it by observation and study, so as to have correct judgment about it. This knowledge is garnered for my own enhancement. It fills what I sense as my inner *emptiness.* My ultimate enhancement is to become *all-knowing,* something that will require a great deal of time by my own efforts while alone. This makes me stingy with my own availability to others. I crave freedom from restraints of commitments, in order to have the time alone to think out what is true and significant. I believe I will be worthwhile as a person when I have attained great inner resources of knowledge and correct judgment about reality. Only then will I feel sure enough of myself to share with others the truth I know. For me as a Five, *to be is to be knowing.*

Eights seek control of the world by arrogance, and Twos seek this by pride. As a Five, however, I seek control over outer reality by the passion of *stinginess*. This is an inordinate attachment to building up my own resources irrespective of the needs of others, and a inordinate disinclination to give away what I possess.

My avoidance as a Five is *emptiness*. I have a craving to know more than I will ever say to others. My self-fulfillment consists in possessing a storehouse of knowledge for myself, so that I am not stupid. What I see as making me important is that I am knowing. I consider my detachment and isolation from others as the means to this superiority and special worth. For me aloofness is great virtue, because I see I need it to become an all-knowing person.

"I am smaller than the world"

If I have a self-concept of being smaller than the world, I identify myself with one of the STUBBORN types: the One, Seven, and Four. I see my fulfillment as centered on what is outside myself, on the effect I have on my environment.

ONE: Aggressive and Stubborn

As a One, I have chosen *aggressive behavior* to achieve my self-fulfillment. I move against the world with a critical attitude of *what should be*. I take pride in being hard-working for the purpose of correcting what is wrong and doing what is right. For me, *to be is to be perfect*. I need perfection in order to stand out as a person of worth.

Within myself, I hear an *inner critic* checking up on how I have been in the past, to make sure I correct whatever I did wrong, or failed to do right. I take on a stance of being exacting not only of myself, but also of others. Often, however, I do not confront the other because I feel that person should know what is lacking, and should be making an effort to correct his or her faults.

As a One, I tend to be *resentful*. This resentment constitutes my ego-fixation. It is *a feeling of indignant displeasure because exterior reality is not the way it should be*. I impose my own standards of perfection on others with an exacting stubbornness. When things are not the way I think they should be, I am annoyed and resentful. At the same time, I avoid acknowledging this resentment, or *anger*, because I am trying to be perfect, and I would consider anger to be a fault. Not only is anger my avoidance, but it is also my specific passion. As a result it is doubly difficult for me to see anger as my predominant fault. I have a compulsion to deny I am ever angry.

SEVEN: Compliant and Stubborn

As a Seven, I express my self-concept of being smaller than the world by moving toward the world in *compliant behavior*. My ego-fixation is *planning*. I see my fulfillment as living in a cheerful world. Since often my environment is not cheerful, I make plans for cheerful happenings with others. As long as my environment is not cheerful and exciting I will feel unfulfilled, and so I will make more and more plans such that I have a wealth of opportunities for a cheerful and exciting life. It seems to me as a Seven that there is always room in my life for more happenings.

My pride as a Seven is being *nice*. This means particularly that I share my contagious enjoyment of life by being entertaining. I focus on the bright side of life, and talk away pain and discomfort. For me, *to be is to be cheerful.*

My specific avoidance is *pain.* I am uncomfortable with persons who are serious or distressed. Since I think my fulfillment is attained through cheerful surroundings, I do not want life to have pain and distress.

As a Seven, my passion is *over-indulgence.* I tend to escape from pain and tension through intemperance. I do not see this passion as a vice, because pleasures make life cheerful and exciting, and they alleviate pain and tension. In my estimation, if some pleasure is good, more is better. For this reason, I will tend to think that the excess of pleasure, called over-indulgence, can be conducive to my fulfillment.

Just as Ones are experienced as stubborn persons in their exacting stance toward others, as a Seven I am stubborn in my insistence that life be fun. I impose on others this kind of behavior, though in a nice way, and make others feel guilty about taking life seriously, or being sad because of some loss. My insistence on cheerfulness will strike others as superficiality, as though I am not in touch with reality, or am simply idealistic to a fault.

FOUR: Detached and Stubborn

As a Four, I have the ego-fixation of *melancholy,—* a "sweet regret for what has been lost." I tend to dwell excessively on past tragedy and think that such *moodiness* makes me special because of what I have gone through. I feel I have real life only when I am going through a whole spectrum of emotions. Like the One and the Seven, I have a self-concept of being smaller than the world and see my fulfillment in having an effect on my surroundings with my own personality. While Ones want to set things right in outside reality, and Sevens want to make their environment cheerful, as a Four I want to create in outside reality the expression of my own unique feelings and refinement. I believe I have experienced life in depths that others are incapable of appreciating, or even perceiving. As a result I often feel others do not understand me. I intuitively pick up the feelings of others with such sensitivity that I may not even know if these feelings are mine or those of others.

As a Four, I see my fulfillment in being creative in the expression of my own unique person. To me, it does not suffice that I have stored my refinement within myself. To me fulfillment depends on my refinement being known and experienced by others. For me, *to be is to be unique.* I seek to express my own sentiments and refinement in symbols. Often this is through one of the arts, but it also may be in the way I adorn my own room. Just as Ones formulate in their own minds how their environment should be and Sevens make plans that their environment have cheerful happenings, as a Four I *rehearse* how I want to express my deepest feelings before others.

Like Ones and Sevens, as a Four I am *stubborn* in insisting on how the environment is to be. Whereas Ones insist on adherence to their own standards of what is correct and incorrect, and Sevens insist on life being cheerful, as a Four I impose my own *taste,* though in doing that I may simply withdraw from whatever is distasteful to me. Others may complain about the stubbornness of my temperament, as in the following anecdote about the artistic temperament of liturgists:

> Q. "What is the difference between a terrorist and a liturgist?"

A. "You can negotiate with a terrorist."

As a Four, my passion is *envy*. This is a resentment toward those whose striking personality is seen as lessening my own worth. Since I see my fulfillment in being superior to others in the way I express my unique feelings and good taste, I may experience the striking personality of another creative person as diminishing my own worth.

"I must adjust to the world"

If I have decided that to be fulfilled I must adjust to the world as it is, I will identify myself with the Three, Six or Nine. Since the fall from society was occasioned by the world being experienced as alienating to my deepest desires, I am in an ambiguous situation of conforming to that alienating world to achieve my self-worth. As a consequence, others will experience me as SELF-ABSORBED. I will be excessively preoccupied with myself, because I am trying to achieve fulfillment from a world often alien to my deepest yearnings.

THREE: Aggressive and Self-absorbed

As a Three, I have chosen to use *aggressive behavior* in conforming to society as it is. My ego-fixation is *vainglory: the presentation of an image of myself before others designed to gain esteem for myself.* The public esteem that I want for my own fulfillment is seen by me as earned by my *achievements*. My goal in life is success. What I see as "success" is not obtained simply by attaining my goals. To me, success means that others give me esteem for what I have accomplished. I will tend to value and justify whatever brings me such recognition.

Because I identify my personal worth with my accomplishments, I will be inclined to say and do whatever will present a good image of myself in the eyes of others. As a consequence, my specific passion is *deceit: the attitude of seeking to persuade others to believe what in fact is not true.* In the final instance, what I really value are *appearances.* I only feel fulfilled when others see me as successful.

Since no one success is likely to keep me feeling esteemed by others, in my continued quest for fulfillment I will *crave* one success after another. The greatest evil for me will be failure, since it is failure that will shame me, or make me feel guilty or worthless. That is why *failure* is that which I avoid above all else. For me as a Three, *to be is to be successful.*

My success-oriented compulsion as a Three can release great energy because my chosen behavior pattern is moving against the world. It is by aggression that I seek achievements. Moving against others makes me highly competitive as a person. In my aggressivity, I may feel justified in taking advantage of others. After all, the achievement of success establishes in my view what I consider to be my worth as a person. Ambition to me is great virtue, and I view the lack of ambition as great vice.

As a Three I need to admit that this seeking a good image in an alienating world causes me to be self-absorbed. I have to adjust myself to cut a good figure. Such self-absorption is often noticed in my penchant to boast about my achievements. Even the way I carry my body and the way I dress to attract attention may suggest boastfulness and a preoccupation with myself.

SIX: Compliant and Self-absorbed

As a Six, I also am a self-absorbed person because I strive to adjust myself to the world as it is in order to achieve fulfillment. Instead of moving against the world aggressively, however, I have a compliant behavior. I am dependent on how the world already is, which I perceive as making great demands on me. This makes me *apprehensive*. I feel a great need to be cautious lest I make a mistake, and thus not respond properly to what is demanded of me.

For me as a Six, it is very difficult to make decisions. I am very unsure of myself, and do not readily trust my own judgment in what to do or not do. The only way I will feel secure is by some authority outside myself making decisions for me. I see my fulfillment as a good person in adjusting my behavior in loyalty to the authority to which I am bound by my membership in a group or by my responsibility to society. For me as a Six, *to be is to be responsible*. What I avoid above all is *deviance*.

My ego-fixation is *cowardice,* which is defined as *a lack of resolution*. Because the anxiety of my self-doubt causes me to be afraid to act on the basis of my own free decisions, my specific passion is *fear*, that is, *an attitude of insecurity because of perceived threats to one's well-being*. As a Six, I accept being fearful and apprehensive as conducive to my fulfillment, since to lack such fear and apprehension would leave me unguarded in the midst of possible threats to my security.

Just as Threes are self-absorbed in their *boastfulness*, so I, as a Six, am self-absorbed by my *caution*. I so much fear making a mistake that I cannot rely only on my own judgment.

NINE: Detached and Self-absorbed

As a Nine, my ego-fixation is *indolence: the disinclination for focused activity.* Through indulging in small comforts, I am easily distracted from doing my job. Just as Threes are fearful of losing their *dignity* by failure and Sixes are fearful of losing their *security* by relying on their own judgment, so as a Nine I am afraid of losing my *inner tranquillity* by involvement.

As a Nine, I seek my fulfillment by detachment from outer reality. I move away from the world in order to find inner peace, wherein I find my fulfillment. For me as a Nine, *to be is to be content.* I have a strategy of withdrawal from any kind of tension that may threaten my contentment. What I avoid above all is *conflict.*

My ruling passion as a Nine is *laziness: the attitude of taking things easy.* I see taking things easy as virtuous, because it is means for me to withdraw from tensions and to experience being content. Just as Threes are self-absorbed by vainglory, and Sixes are self-absorbed by apprehension, so, as a Nine, I am self-absorbed in being easy-going. To maintain my inner contentment I will be wary of involvements which could demand of me a lot of effort and responsibility.

12. THE THREE CENTERS[1]

According to the enneagram system, the human psyche has three functions: instinct, feeling and thinking. These are also called "centers," and are represented by the terms of GUT—HEART—HEAD, as follows:

- The *gut center*, or instinctive function, operates with spontaneity. Operating out of instinct is like operating out of habit. When my body presence operates from my gut center, I interact with the world with the implied statement: "Here I am; deal with me."

- The *heart center*, or feeling function, interacts with the hearts of others. It recognizes and appreciates being loved and esteemed. When my body presence operates from my heart center, I interact with the world with the implied statement: "I want others to like me a lot."

- The *head center*, or thinking function, is reflective and deliberative. It concerns knowing where everything or everyone is, including myself in the mix. When my body presence operates from my head center, I interact with the world with the implied statement: "I wonder how all this fits together, and where I fit in."

In the process of selecting one of the nine personality types as my way to be a person, I have at the same time

---

[1] Beesing, M., *et al., op. cit.,* pp. 141-155.

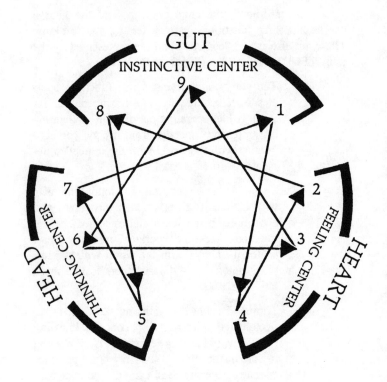

The Three Centers

chosen one of the three centers as my "preferred center." According to enneagram theory, especially as expounded by George Gurdjieff,[2] I become unbalanced by this choice of making one of the centers my preferred way of being a person. To function in a balanced way I should use each center of functioning according to what is appropriate for the situation:

- When playing ball, I should be immersed in my *gut center*, trusting that the body will react spontaneously to stimuli, just as a trained dog leaps instinctively to catch a ball.

- In personal encounter, I should operate out of my *heart center,* so that I am sensitive to the feelings of others, and sense how to give and receive love.

- When making decisions, I should deliberate with my *head center,* in order to choose the good through accurate perception and reflection.

Substituting for a Neglected Function

In my fall from society, I chose one center as preferred, to the neglect of the other centers. I use my preferred way of functioning to substitute for the functioning of the neglected centers. Because of this, something in my behavior will be lacking in essential humanness:

- If I use my *gut center* in personal encounter instead of my *heart center*, I will lack a sensitivity to personal intimacy and tend to impose myself on others.

---

[2] Cf Pyotr D. Ouspensky, *In Search of the Miraculous,* Hartcourt, Brace & World, New York, 1949.

- If I use my *gut center* for making decisions instead of my *head center*, my decisions are apt to be biased rather than objective.

- If, in playing ball, I use my *heart center* instead of my *gut center*, I may insert into the game a disturbing concern about how we are relating or feeling about one another.

- If I use my *heart center* for making decisions instead of using my *head center*, I may be led into pure sentimentality.

- To use my *head center* for playing ball is to lose the spontaneity needed by an athlete. To use my *head center* for meeting people will hinder me from being concerned whether or not I am liked.

Differentiation of the Nine Types

As shown in the last chapter, in the early development of my ego-consciousness as separate from the world, I made a choice between three self-concepts vis-à-vis the world: INDEPENDENT, STUBBORN, and SELF-ABSORBED. It is noteworthy that each of these self-concepts is expressed in types of a different preferred center, as follows:

INDEPENDENT: Eight (gut), Two (heart), Five (head).

STUBBORN: One (gut), Four (heart), Seven (head).

SELF-ABSORBED: Nine (gut), Three (heart), Six (head).

This suggests that already as a child I had an inborn inclination to one preferred center. When I formed my ego by a self-concept, it was natural to express this self-concept in that preferred center, and so the corresponding personality type emerged.

Another way of differentiation the nine types according to the three centers is to see how the three types *within each center* are distinguished from each other. To do this it is helpful to consider our enneagram theory regarding "wings" and "denial points."

The concept of WINGS is used when an enneagram point is on the edge of its own preferred center, and thus adjacent to another center. In that case, the personality functions well not only in the preferred center, but also in the adjacent center. That adjacent center is called a "wing." Even though in each case there is a preferred center, the wing function is also chosen for ordinary use, something like the secondary function in Jungianism, but without distinguishing between dealing with the outside world and the inside world. The third enneagram center, however, is not integrated into the personality, but the function of the preferred center is substituted for the function of this neglected third center.

The concept of DENIAL POINTS is used when the personality point is not adjacent to another center. This is the case with the Three, Six, and Nine. When there is no wing, the preferred center substitutes its functioning for the functioning of the other two centers.

By using the theory of wings and denial points, the three types within each center readily become distinguished as different personalities, as follows:

GUT CENTER
Eight: wing in the head center
Nine: no wing
One: wing in the heart center

HEART CENTER
Two: wing in the gut center
Three: no wing
Four: wing in the head center

HEAD CENTER
Five: wing in the heart center
Six: no wing
Seven: wing in the gut center

In considering the differentiation of the nine types according to the three functions, I will begin with those enneagram points with wings:

Points with Wings

Gut Persons: ONE & EIGHT

If I am a ONE, I am a gut-person with a wing in my heart center. I am a *feeling gut-person*. Not only do I function well by *instinct*, but also with *feeling*. By instinct I will impose myself in a situation, but also I will be concerned in my heart that others like me a lot.

As a ONE, however, I abstain from using my *head center*, and I tend to substitute instinctive functioning for thinking. Substituting instinct for thinking causes me to "think" with a personal bias. I tend to *impose* my own thinking on others, without asking how they see the situation. I impose my "truth" on them. The "perfection" I insist on as a One originates mainly from my own point of view.

If I am an EIGHT, I am a gut-person with a wing in my head center. I am a *thinking gut-person*. I am distinguished by functioning well not only by *instinct*, but also in *thinking*. By instinct I impose myself on others, but I also like to think about how everything fits together, and what is the significance of everything.

As an EIGHT, however, I substitute instinct for *feeling*, such that I consider I am relating well with others when I make a statement to them. Because I neglect the use of my heart center, I do not have much concern as to whether or not others like me. I think the way to relate well with others is to make them deal with me.

Heart Persons: TWO & FOUR

If I am a TWO, I am a heart-person with a wing in my gut center. I am a *instinctive heart-person*. I am distinguished by functioning well not only in *feeling* but also by *instinct*. Not only do I seek relationships of the heart, but also I impose myself.

As a TWO, however, I neglect my thinking function, and substitute feeling for *thinking*. Because I neglect thinking, I am not interested much in how everything fits together. I restrict my interest to what is going on in the lives of my favorite persons. The substitution of feeling for thinking is also shown when I insist that my special other can do no wrong, like the case of a mother insisting that her son is a good boy, even though he may be in jail.

If I am a FOUR, I am a heart-person with a wing in my head center. I am a *thinking heart-person*. I am distinguished by functioning well not only with *feeling* but also with *thinking*. As a Four, I concentrate on relationships of the heart, but also I am interested in the world at large, especially the world of culture.

As a Four, however, I fall short in instinctive functioning, and I tend to substitute feeling for *instinct*. Because of this, I lack spontaneity. By rehearsing, I seek to make my body presence express my unique feelings and good taste, instead of simply being casual and "going with the flow." As a result, I have a *studied charm,* and others may wonder what is behind my smile.

Head Persons: FIVE & SEVEN

If I am a FIVE, I am a head-person with a wing in my heart center. I am a *feeling head-person.* I am distinguished by functioning well not only by *thinking,* but also with *feeling* and sensitivity to others. Not only do I use thinking to know what is going on and how I fit in, but also I seek relationships of the heart.

As a FIVE, however, I substitute thinking for *instinct.* I lack spontaneity. I tend to reflect and deliberate before reacting to outer stimuli. This may cause me to freeze in crisis situations, and will produce a certain awkwardness in playing sports.

If I am a SEVEN, I am a head-person with a wing in my gut center. I am an *instinctive head-person.* I am distinguished by functioning well not only in *thinking* but also by *instinct.* Not only do I live in my ideas and plans, but also I impose myself on others.

As a SEVEN, however, I substitute thinking for the *feeling function,* with the result that I seek escape from personal intimacy by having people fit into the happenings I have planned. I fail to ask how others feel about being asked to my party. I project my cheerfulness on others, and do not readily notice the pain of the real world. My idealism can cause me to overlook the reality of life as experienced by others.

Denial Points

We are left with the three denial points: the Nine, Three, and Six. The term "denial" is applied to these three types for several reasons. First of all, they tend to deny they have a problem. If my personality type has a wing, I will eventually become aware that I have a problem:

- As a One, I will sense that I am imposing on others my own point of view.

- As a Two, I will notice that I lack interests beyond certain relationships that I have.

- As a Four, I may be discontented with my lack of spontaneity.

- As a Five, I will notice I do poorly in sports, or feel inferior at cocktail parties.

- As a Seven, I will notice that others are disappointed by my fleeing from intimacy.

- As an Eight, I will learn that I trample on the feelings of another.

Why, however, will I deny I have a problem if I am a Nine, Three, or Six? If my type is at a denial point, I will tend to deny I have a problem because *I am not really in touch with myself.* I do not know myself. Why is this? It is because I deny the functioning of the preferred center I have chosen. This is, in fact, the main reason that the Nine,

Three, and Six are called denial points. As a Nine, Three, or Six, the center I have chosen as my preferred function is not being used by me for its proper functioning. I am indeed using it, but only as a substitute for the other two functions. This explanation may sound gratuitous as well as subtle, but let us see how this theory works out as applied to each of the denial points:

NINE

As a Nine, I have chosen my gut center as my preferred center. Nevertheless, people would hardly call me "gutsy." I am actually *lackadaisical*. I do not do things with gusto like the other two gut-persons:

- Were I an Eight, I would have great energy for initiative; I would enjoy confrontation, and anything that would call upon my strength as a person.

- Were I a One, I would take pride in being a meticulous, hard worker; I would be willing to put out enormous energy on details.

Why my lack of energy as a Nine? It is because I am not in touch with the inner vitality of my instinctive functioning. The gut center is my preferred center, but I use it only to substitute in situations calling for functioning from the heart center or head center. I use instinct only to substitute for feeling and for thinking.

What does it mean to *substitute instinct for the feeling function*? Obviously, instead of seeking to be liked and to be sensitive to the feelings of others, I simply plant myself. I use my instinct in the sense of being comfortable with the camaraderie of my old friends, but I do not move out to make new friends, nor take pains to make myself attractive so that others will like me. I like to be easy-going and planted wherever I am. At the same time, I will let others draw me out into activities, and often I am hoping they will do so.

By *substituting instinct for thinking* as a Nine, I am content with very limited interests, such as collecting things, puttering around, or watching TV. I like routine, where I do not have to use energy to think much about what I have to do. In other words, I like to live by habit, rather than by gaining new ideas and interests.

THREE

As a Three I have chosen my heart center as my preferred center. Nevertheless, I do not make matters of the heart the primary interest in my life, as do Twos and Fours:

- Were I a Two, caring about the feelings of another would be my primary concern.

- Were I a Four, caring about my own feelings would be my primary concern.

As a Three, however, I put my own feelings in a sack, and I see my fulfillment in terms of success as being more important to me than how others feel. When what is personal comes up I may consider it a *distraction* from being efficient in my task. Yes, I do care whether or not others like me, but I assume that they will esteem me only if I have achievements. I have denied the proper use of my preferred center. I do use it however, to substitute feeling both for thinking and for instinct.

How do I use my feeling center *to substitute for thinking*? One way is by limiting my quest for knowing to what will help me be successful. I value knowledge to the extent that it promotes the success of my undertakings.

How do I use my feeling center *to substitute for instinct*? As a Three, I confront others with feelings that seem sincere but really are deceiving. I put on an appearance that will cause others to respond favorably to what I am promoting. What appears to be spontaneity really comes from a tactic to win over the person to my own advantage.

SIX

As a Six, I have chosen my head center as my preferred center. Nevertheless, I do not become stimulated by doing a lot of thinking such as happens with Fives and Sevens:

- Were I a Five, I would get excited by new ideas.

- Were I Seven, I would get excited by new plans.

As a Six, however, I tend to avoid acquiring new knowledge. I feel most secure from the knowledge I already have of what is demanded of me. I want my knowledge to give me security, but to do that for me as a Six, the knowledge must not change. I block out new knowledge because I fear it will make life too demanding. Probably I do not read much, nor do I attend workshops. The reason is that by knowing more I may add to the burden of my responsibilities, and lessen the security I have from what I know from the past.

As a Six, I use thinking *to replace feeling*. The performance of my duties has priority over relating with people. I consider that doing my duty for others, such as for my family, is an adequate demonstration of my love and care. By this others can *know* I love them. It may not occur to me as a Six that the expression of affection is crucial for communicating love to others.

As a Six, I also use thinking *to substitute for instinct.* Instead of being spontaneous in my bodily expression, there is a rigidity in my movement. Since in my thinking I am ruled by responsibility and loyalty, I will insist at meetings that everything be done according to the rules and agenda, and I may fail to appreciate what occurs spontaneously.

Conclusion

Of what use is all this analysis of preferred centers and wings? The answer is twofold:

- By seeing the nine types emerging from the centers, we can understand better why people of each type think and act the way they do.

- By this analysis of non-use and misuse of our functions or centers, we will see better what kind of *healing* is needed to restore our wholeness.

In short, these theories about the three centers show that the cause of our personality problem is not from some evil inside ourselves, but rather because we are *unbalanced.* To be thrown off balance can create a problem, as we can recognize in the case of an automatic washing machine. The machine gets spinning again when the balance of the clothes is restored. In a somewhat analogous way, to restore the balance of the three functions of my personality can create for me a new life. It may not be a simple matter for me to correct the balance once I am habituated to unbalanced functioning, but before I will even do anything to overcome my compulsion I must first know I have a problem.

What I have been doing in Section B of this book up to now is *to uncover a problem*. Hopefully this has been done, and the reader is now interested in knowing how to *overcome the problem*. There is always a risk in giving people answers to questions they do not have, or to try to fill in a hole when there is none. I have tried to dig a hole, to present a problem. Granted that I have done that, let us begin to fill it up again by studying the kinds of conversion necessary to transform a compulsed personality into a redeemed personality.

13. INSTINCTUAL CONVERSION[1]

Once I have ascertained my own specific point on the enneagram figure, I am ready to begin my spiritual journey to live a more balanced life. The pathway of this journey begins by moving against the arrow of compulsion. This may be called "instinctual conversion," because it is a turning around of my instinctual energy by moving against the instinct of compulsion.

Since such action does restore more balance to my being, with practice it will tend to "feel right" as I stretch myself to take on a new personality. Due to the fact that the abiding Spirit of God works with me, and gives me both the desire and the power of attaining a redeemed personality, in moving against the arrow I may often have a sense of spiritual well-being called "consolation." In other words, it feels good to be good.

Consolation/Desolation

Just as passionate love as lived in my specific passion produces good feelings because what I yearn for in my distorted sense of reality is viewed as being attained, so, too, when I attain a certain conscious liberation from my prevailing compulsion by going against the arrow of compulsion, I begin to perceive a certain satisfaction not only in my mind but also in my instinctual nature. This satisfaction is called a "consolation" and it is experienced in a specific way in each enneagram type. St. Ignatius of Loyola uses the following terms to describe spiritual consolations: "being on fire," "being thankful," "peace," "delight," and "strength."

---

[1] Cf Beesing, et al., pp. 134-141, 158-171, 199-210.

Opposite to consolation, is what St. Ignatius calls *desolation*, such as "turmoil," "darkness," "restlessness," and "despair." Because of such negative feelings, along with faintheartedness or self-doubt, I could be led to move in the opposite direction. Such *moving with the arrow* will have the result that I compound my problem by also taking on the ego-fixation of the enneagram type pointed to by the arrow. This could happen because not only do I not try to move against the arrow, but I give up even trying to live the pride characteristic of my own compulsion. Something discourages me from believing in myself. I give up thinking I can do anything worthwhile. Even the discovery of my enneagram type could be a cause of rejecting myself because of the flawed motivation I see in myself.

An Ascetical Effort

Going against the arrow of compulsion is an *ascetical effort*. As I try to move against the current of instinctual energy generated by passionate love, I will begin to feel the real force of this instinctual energy. To move against the arrow of compulsion will not be easy, nor will it "feel right," because the compulsion is instinctive and to move against it is not instinctive. I will need conscious energy and determination of will to do this, but it is within my own power to do so. Having been enlightened about my compulsion through the discovery of my enneagram type, I can now put to use this light by taking on the principle of Ignatian spirituality called "*agere contra*,", i.e., "acting against." In Ignatius it means acting against disordered affections in my own nature. Here I use it as acting against the instinct of compulsion.

We will study the ascetical effort needed for instinctual conversion by taking up the enneagram points according to the three sets of *aggressive types* (8, 3, 1), *compliant types* (2, 6, 7), and *detached types* (5, 9, 4). The key to understanding this movement of going *against the arrow* is my taking on the *pride* of the type toward which I move. I want to identify myself consciously with that pride, and have it replace the pride of my own enneagram point.

In taking on the pride of this other enneagram point, I do not become that personality type. I remain my original personality type, but it will no longer be driven and justified by that old pride. As a result my personality will be considerably less compulsive.

Aggressive Types (8, 3, 1)

If I am one of the aggressive types, Eight, Three, or One, I need to move against the arrow by moving toward *compliant behavior*. As I take on the pride of the opposite type, I will move toward the world as it is, and become more accepting and receiving.

On the other hand, if I as an aggressive type move *with the arrow*, I will take on the ego-fixation of a *detached type*. It is very unhealthy for an aggressive personality to become detached and withdraw from activity in the world. It would compound my compulsiveness.

EIGHT—>Two ("I am helpful")

My instinctual conversion as an EIGHT involves giving up the ego-consciousness of identifying my goodness with being a strong, powerful person. In its place, I move against the arrow of compulsion by taking on the pride of the Two, who says, "I am helpful." This means I make an effort to be proud of serving the needs of another. This will not feel right to me,—at least initially,—because it is going against the instinct of compulsion. However, I do have the power to attend to the needs of another, and to take pride in doing so by saying, "I am good because I am helpful." It is a matter of laying down my life to become sensitive to the need of another who is special in my life. This is to give up being cantankerous and violent, for aggressivity hurts rather than heals. At the same time I should see that it takes great inner strength to be a caregiver.

In this way, my personality as an Eight will be softened. I will be moving into my neglected heart center, and this inclines me to see others before I see myself. I will now be asking the questions: "Will others like me or not?" and "How can I make others like me?" Instead of asserting myself, I will seek to please the other.

As an Eight, I can never actually become a Two. It is of course possible to move into flattery and catering to others, but even attending to another in excess will be less harmful to me as an Eight than the status quo of charging into others with the pride of being strong. In attending to the need of another, I will not be giving up being strong, but I will be challenged to recognize my own tenderness as a value. After all, I had simply repressed my soft side, and it still remained within me. A lot of my toughness was put on to hide the marshmallow inside.

By seeking to please by service to others, I will get in touch with the tapped-up energy of my heart center. Eventually it will come to feel good to be tender. In times of stress, however, I will need extra determination to attend to the needs of another, rather than revert to the aggressive strategy of the Eight for defense. I may discover, to my surprise, that loving another with tenderness often means "giving in," i.e., submitting to what pleases the other. Instead of simply imposing myself on others, I will begin adapting myself to their actual feelings and desires. This, of course, is to come a long way on my journey of self-transformation. In place of insisting that I get *respect*, I seek to give *service*.

In this change of my personality by giving up my pride in being a strong person and taking on the pride of being helpful, I may discover the consolation of the gift of tears, because I feel deeply grateful for having discovered that in spite of all my efforts "to tough it out" in life I am really soft and tender inside. I will find that I am loved with affection and appreciation for the service I have rendered to others. The world outside me does love me. I am esteemed not so much because I am tough, but more because I have understood the deep needs of others and have served them from my heart.

If instead I should be plunged into self-doubt and discouragement because of becoming aware of my character defects as an Eight, or because of too much resistance from others, I might give up activity and move *with the arrow* to the ego-stinginess of the Five. I now would prize being alone, and no longer have confidence I can overcome my opponents. Such flight from struggle would lead me to selfishness, and a sense of worthlessness. I would have compounded my compulsion as an Eight with the compulsion of the Five. It is really bad for me to become merely an observer of life.

THREE—>Six ("I am loyal.")

As a THREE, I am invited to give up my ego-consciousness of being good because I am successful, and to move *against the arrow* of compulsion to take on the pride of the Six, who characteristically says, "I am loyal." Of course, it will not feel right to identify myself with the interests and rules of a group, because I am so independent-minded that I always think of myself as the leader. Being accustomed to being the one in charge, I will by nature expect others to follow me and be loyal to me at all costs. However, as a Three I do have the capacity to let go of the idea that I am good when I am successful, and replace it by taking pride in being loyal to the norms of the group to which I belong.

By going against the arrow, I commit myself to comply with the responsibilities of being a good team member, and to live for the common good of social reality. It means that I give up being so aggressive, and instead I adjust myself to comply with the moral demands that are common to all members of my group. I will take pride in identifying with what is good for society, rather that what will bring *acclaim* to myself. I do not relinquish my abilities for achievement, but I unite these achievements with those of others instead of competing with them. Rather than seek my own advantage, I join with others for the betterment of society.

By taking on the compliance of the Six, I will awaken my untapped head center. I will begin to see the bigger picture. Instead of being so self-absorbed that I restrict my quest for knowing to what will advance my success, I open myself to know how everything fits together, and how I fit into everything.

By saying with pride that I am *loyal* I include a special place in my heart for family and friends. I see now that friendship is a great good in itself. Perhaps as a compulsed Three I tended to see friendship mainly to be a stepping stone to my own success, and so I sought friends who would be *useful* to me. Now I see that true friendship is to be for the other in faithfulness. Here I begin to unlock my preferred heart center in yearning to live a shared life in a shared world.

Once I become more engaged with others in shared projects and shared life, I may experience the spiritual consolation of *joy*. Joy is like each of us playing our own instrument in a symphony orchestra, and feeling we are all together. In making my life a contribution to a common project for the common good, I become much more immune to despair when I suffer failure or for some reason am unable to work, since good is being done even if I am not doing it. Even in retirement, I can feel fulfilled by being like the setting sun, as I smile warmly on all those busy doing many good things, while I simply praise them and give encouragement.

On the other hand, as a Three I could lose my self-esteem when I come to see that the true motivation of all my work has been self-seeking and vanity. This could cause me to turn my aggressivity against myself, and move *with the arrow* to the ego-indolence of the Nine. Such a self-destructive attitude might also come from the shock of failure. In moving as a Three to the indolence typical the Nine's compulsion, I do not end up as an easy-going person, but rather I experience the desolation of restlessness and inner turmoil.

ONE—>Seven ("I am nice.")

As a compulsed ONE, I lived in a divided house. My inner critic inhabited the main part of the house, but down in the cellar anything might be going on. I expected that all my underlying feelings and desires were to give an account to the inner critic upstairs, but these feelings and desires did seem to have a life of their own. At times I felt like a dormant volcano that might erupt at any time. When I saw others following their base desires I was resentful. After all, they should be avoiding bad conduct.

To overcome this divided house as a One, I needed to develop a much greater trust in what goes on in my cellar, and to pay less attention to the inner critic upstairs. That inner critic was not the voice of my conscience. As a child I had internalized the critical voice of others, especially parent figures. I needed to befriend all the parts of my being. The scriptures themselves indicate that there is no poison inside of me, not even in my base parts. As the Book of Wisdom states:

> God...fashioned all things that they might have being;
> and the creatures of the world are wholesome,
> in them no fatal poison can be found.[2]

I came to realize that within my deep well is to be found the presence of God, and I am continually coming forth into existence from God's creative power. Somehow I need more trust in my inner instincts as favorable to my good. Perhaps my own judgment is biased. I need to listen not only to the deeper parts of my being, but also to the voices of friends who want me to be less serious and less aggressive. They see me as having repressed good parts of my being, such as the part which wants to have fun. Perhaps they have tried to get me to take myself less seriously by teasing me.

Most likely I grew up very responsible for others, and early on locked up my inner child which yearns to have fun. All the "shoulds" in my life repressed my childlike

---

[2] Ws 1:14

spontaneity, but it was still somewhere inside me. How can I now let out that inner child?

Overcoming the critical voice of the inner critic is greatly helped by moving *against the arrow* to the pride of the Seven, who says, "I am nice." To be nice means to be entertaining. As a One, I need to give up my pride in being hardworking, and instead concentrate on being more entertaining like a Seven. One way of being entertaining is to develop my sense of humor. There is a great deal to see as funny in life. My body itself is ridiculously funny in its sexuality. So is my insistence that everything should be in its place, and my binding myself by so many "shoulds." Am I not rather silly in being so fussy and picky?

Shifting my attitude so that I take pride by being *nice* like a Seven results in my getting much more acquainted with my neglected head center. It is the head center that can acquire a sense of the ridiculous. It is also the head center that can focus on the bright side of life. An example of this is a story from the Fathers of the Desert. Two anchorites, one elderly and the other youthful, were leaving Alexandria on the way back to their hermitages in the desert after several days on the town. The young anchorite was lamenting about what hypocrites they were, pretending to be holy men in the desert and then indulging themselves as randy men in Alexandria. The old man replied that it is true they had fallen into sinful pleasures but they would return now to their life of penance much the wiser about their weaknesses and their need for God's mercy. The young anchorite remained restless and soon left the desert. He fell into a dissolute life in the city. The old man continued on in his life as a hermit and died in holiness. He is remembered as one of the saints in the church calendar.

169

Like the old anchorite, as a One I need to avoid post-mortems and bewailing my past sins. To turn anger on myself can cause depression, and to turn it on others is to put them down. By taking on the pride of the Seven, I can defuse much pent-up anger and become a great lover of people. Seeking to be pleasant and entertaining will, at any rate, make me much easier to live with. I do have the inner resources to be this way, while at the same time not losing the great positive qualities of my Oneness.

The consolation I can receive by moving into the pride of the Seven is *peace of soul*. By becoming deaf to the voice of the inner critic, that voice will become much less strident. The attitude of the Seven is that, even if there is disorder, everything can still be okay, for I can be nice to people and we can enjoy being together. Like a Seven I can say, "The more, the merrier!"

On the other hand, should I feel as a One that I have so much to do that I cannot do anything right, I may decide to stop trying, and move *with the arrow* toward the ego-melancholy of the Four. To become inactive and detached as a One will not make me happy. I need involvement for any sort of satisfaction in life. I will not feel enriched by becoming moody, but instead I may fall into the desolation of restlessness.

Compliant Types (2, 6, 7)

If I am a compliant type,—a Two, Six, or Seven,— I am to seek instinctual conversion by moving *against the arrow,* and taking on *withdrawing behavior.* Instead of depending on the world for fulfillment I become *detached.*

Discouragement and stress could cause me instead to move *with the arrow* of compulsion, so that I take on the ego-fixation of an a*ggressive type.* This will compound my problem because I will become an angry person.

TWO—>Four ("I am unique")

As a TWO, I am called to instinctual conversion by moving *against the arrow* to take on the pride of the Four, who says, "I am unique." By nature Fours know the importance of doing things just to satisfy their own inclinations. As a Two, by appreciating myself as a special and unique person, I can come to value doing some things just for myself, even though I used to think I was wasting time when not doing something helpful to another.

As a Two, I need to refrain from adapting myself to please others, and instead concentrate on being appreciated for my own *feelings.* Like the Four, I need to believe I am special because of the emotions I have experienced in life. I need to let the true feelings of my heart be known by sharing how I really am, and how I have felt in the past. Thereby I will be become conscious of my heart center as *receiving love,* instead of always trying to *get love.* It is the expression of love with another through mutual confidences that opens the door to personal communion.

As a Two, I need solitude and meditation. Because of my compulsion to do for another, I have been uneasy about spending time alone in meditation, because such prayer is not doing anything for anybody, except, of course, for myself. The practice of meditation can lead me to notice for the first time the many ways in which God has expressed love for me through what has happened in my life. Tears of gratitude may well up as I see evidence of having been loved by God without my having done anything to earn that love.

On the other hand, as a Two I may be tempted to feel that others are taking advantage of me and robbing me of my independence, such that I move *with the arrow* of compulsion to take on the ego-vengeance of the Eight. I surprise others by suddenly bursting out with temper to drive them away in order to defend my dignity. I could also become vengeful toward a special person in my life because that person did not respond with appreciation to my caring.

Any such anger in me as a Two which is directed against others who I ordinarily want to serve will lead me to depression and desolation. I will always end up turning against myself any aggressivity I express toward others. I could succumb to such darkness that I feel I am no longer able to respond to any need of another.

SIX—> Nine ("I am content")

To attain instinctual conversion as a SIX I need to move *against the arrow* to take on the pride of the Nine, who says, "I am content." Nines take pride in being content with the way things are. By copying the Nine, I can let go of my compliant behavior patterns and have a more de-tached attitude. I can let go of my compulsive conformity to authority, whereby I make keeping rules more important than getting along with others. By appreciating the impor-tance of being content, I will be able to make peace and harmony a priority of my life. I will want to take pride in becoming a peacemaker.

Such a change in conscience involves a conversion from a morality based on *law* to a morality based on *values*. Instead of right and wrong being measured by conformity to authorities and rules, as is the case with a morality of law, a morality of values forms the conscience by transcendent values, such as harmony, peace, and love. Instead of following rules, I need to promote values by living them out in my life, and seeking to get them lived in society. To live a value means to dedicate myself to that which is greater than I am. It is to participate in divinity by taking on divine *attitudes*, rather than to adjust myself to the *demands* of a divine authority. Jesus was talking about the importance of values in morality when he challenged the Pharisees not to neglect "the really important teachings of the Law, such as justice and mercy and honesty."[3]

By taking on the pride of the Nine and saying that *to be is to be content*, I am getting in touch with my neglected gut center. I can stop worrying how I fit in, which is typical of my preferred head center, and make people deal with my body presence, as is typical of the gut center. Thereby I can become more self-assured. By affirming that I am a good person because I am content with myself and others, I imitate the Nine's stance that "I am okay and you are okay."

Being content will include letting myself be spontaneous in any situation, trusting that my reactions will be acceptable however they are. By this I will become more trusting of God as accepting everyone and everything, and loving us simply because we are creatures. I can begin to relate to God as loving me for who I am, rather than because I have done my duty. Such spiritual enlightenment may unlock in me a much more zealous spirit.

On the other hand, the stress of opposition to me as a Six could cause me to compound my compulsion by moving *with the arrow* toward the ego-vanity of the Three, so that I begin to seek success even through deceitful stratagems. I may become so aroused at the threats of others to

---

[3] Mt 23:23

my group that I will not only bad-mouth them, but use un-derhanded means to undermine them. I could take on an idealized role of saving my group by means which are de-ceitful and unjust, while justifying this as a defense of law and tradition.

It would be really very bad for me as a Six to be-come *aggressive*, even though I thought it was for the cause of right. I already have a tendency to divide the world into "them" and "us." I would become even more unbalanced by attacking in an aggressive way my opponents in order to champion my own cause. It is one thing to overcome inner doubts by appeal to an outside authority, but something quite other to use force and manipulation to bring about the triumph of my side. We are reminded here of how those who thought themselves righteous in the Jewish law con-spired to have Jesus crucified by trumped-up charges, and all the while claimed they were serving the cause of God.

SEVEN—>Five ("I am knowing")

As a SEVEN, I am invited to instinctual conver-sion by moving away from dependency on pleasure and excitement, and moving *against the arrow* to take on a more reflective life characteristic of the Five, who takes pride in saying, "I am knowing." Like a Five, I need to seek objec-tive knowledge as the way to fulfillment. Healthy Fives have their feet on the ground, for they work hard to know reality as it is. This attitude is healing for me as a Seven, because it leads me away from *imposing* on reality my own optimism. Many people are in distress. Many life situa-tions do not call for excitement, pleasure, and cheerfulness, because that kind of reaction trivializes what is experienced, or simply runs away from it. I need to walk in the shoes of another, and take satisfaction in knowing life as it really is.

For me as a Seven, this means to take on a more serious demeanor.

As a Seven, I need to draw on the Five's ability to study and reflect on experience so as not to miss something of significance in what is going on. This can help me to move from extroversion to introversion, so that I get in touch with my inner well of wisdom. Through this I can come to experience an inner *detachment* replacing my former compulsiveness in seeking diversions. I become more earnest and thereby feel strengthened. Within myself I may experience a peacefulness not caused by exterior comforts or satisfactions.

On the other hand, it is very dangerous for me as a Seven to go *with the arrow* of compulsion to take on the critical stance of the One, as though I could set the world right by being negative and exacting. Like a One, I would become obsessed with an unrealizable perfection for our imperfect world. This would cause me to lose the optimism typical of a Seven, and take on a moodiness which expresses itself in bitter words about all that is wrong. Such harsh judgments on others will plunge my soul into darkness, even though I fantasize that I have feelings of consolation.

Detached Types (5, 9, 4)

If I am a detached type,—a Five, Nine or Four,— when I seek instinctual conversion by moving *against the arrow*, I will take on *aggressive behavior*. Instead of using withdrawal as my main strategy for self-fulfillment, I will stretch my personality by confronting others.

On the other hand, should excessive stress cause me to move *with the arrow* of compulsion, I will compound my compulsiveness by also taking on the ego-fixation of a *compliant type*. In this way, I will lose hope in myself.

FIVE—>Eight ("I am powerful")

I am called to instinctual conversion as a FIVE by moving *against the arrow* to take on the pride of the Eight, who says, "I am powerful." This call involves making a gift to the outside world of my presence and of my resources. I will have the incentive to do this by letting go of my pride in being *knowing*, and replacing this with pride in being *strong*. I am called to use my *power*, my ability to act with assertiveness and initiative. I can take on the self-confidence of the Eight by having confidence in my inner resources and trusting my gut instincts to react spontaneously when involved with others. Like an Eight, I can take a stance of saying, "Here I am; deal with me."

By modeling myself on the pride of the Eight, I can come to enjoy the battle of life, and no longer fear so much to be bruised or embarrassed. I do have the inner strength to stop being afraid of life, and to enter into relationships which are risky because the outcome cannot be controlled. Making others deal with me will probably entail a considerable change in personality, and initially it will seem awkward and stressful. I need a new boldness to strengthen my inner instincts, and get more in touch with my neglected gut center. To practice this, I could make the resolution to speak up at every group meeting I attend.

Through modeling myself on the pride of the Eight, I can be spurred by conviction and boldness to get involved with the world by challenging it. Although initially such moving against the world may not feel right and be felt as stressful, in the long run it will feel right as I am caught on fire with *zeal* to change the world I have long watched and researched. I may see myself having the call of the prophet to tear down and build up.[4]

On the other hand, a fear of facing life could lead me by move *with the arrow* to take on also the ego-fixation of the Seven. My pitfall as a Five would be to take on this characteristic of the Seven in doing too much planning. As a Five, I am normally realistic, with my feet on the ground, but dislike for my environment could lead me to lose touch with life such that I no longer care to reflect on what can be of some service to others, and I simply withdraw into my own dreams and theories.

As a Five, it is important that I study and reflect on what is significant, and avoid making a lot of plans that I never intend to put into action. Otherwise I could easily dry up my inner well of wisdom, and become less and less able to use my thinking as a way to build bridges of relationship with others. I would become much more selfish and withdrawn.

NINE—>Three ("I am successful")

As a NINE I can work toward instinctual conversion by moving *against the arrow* toward the pride of the Three, who says, "I am successful." As long as I just seek as a Nine to be comfortable, I sell myself short on what I can accomplish, and I will not be able to resolve my lack of self-esteem. Leaving aside the pride of being *easy-going*, and taking on the pride of being *successful*, will lead me as a Nine to become more image-conscious. Asking myself how I can become more liked, I will see the need to cultivate my appearance, and to get others to respond to me.

---

[4] Cf Jer 1:10

Like the success-oriented Three, I need to strengthen my outgoing personality by moving against the world. It is very important how others experience my presence. I will try to take on a head of steam to be brisk, pro-active, cheerful, direct, exciting, and fearless in facing people. Should there be an occasion when I lack the energy to do this in front of others, then I should retire to my private room until I do have the ability to come out and act energetic. After all, my image before others is very important for convincing them to follow me as a leader.

In order to take a stand and make a difference in the world, I will need to be well-organized. I do have the ability to set attainable goals, and to work hard to get things done. When tempted to become easy-going again, I simply need to say that I do not want to "go with the flow" of my compulsion, but to move against it.

After having been resigned for so long to receive little appreciation, I will be surprised to receive love and esteem from others as I take the initiative in enterprising action. This may awaken in my heart center a deep thankfulness for such love, and I will tend to want my love to be of help to others, that they lead more successful lives. I will want my life to make a difference to others.

On the other hand, I could become so aware of my indolence as a Nine that I completely lose hope in myself, such that I move *with the arrow* toward the self-doubt characteristic of the ego-cowardice Six. Having already a lack of self-esteem as a Nine, I would compound my problem by doubting my own judgment of what is right and wrong, and begin to say that I am no good and never will be any good.

178

FOUR—>One ("I am hardworking")

As a FOUR, I am invited to instinctual conversion by moving *against the arrow* to take on the pride of the One, who says, "I am hardworking." Rather than continuing to define myself as good because I are unique and special, I need to model myself on the One by intervening in society with an aggressive stance. By taking pride in working hard, I can find my new identity as a Four in bettering reality outside myself, and making others deal with the values I cherish.

I need to redefine myself as dedicated to transforming outside reality according to my values. To do that requires a dedication to honesty, directness, and hard work. In this way I can get in touch with my neglected gut center. I will be willing to take charge of projects to get the job done, while trying to lead others to be creative in the use of their own talents.

All this will lead me out of moodiness and self-absorption. By dedicating my talents to making the world better, I will find unique inner resources which I can put to use in promoting human development. I may experience the spiritual consolation of being on fire with *zeal*.

My bane as a Four would be to move *with the arrow* to the ego-flattery characteristic of the Two. As a Four, I could fall into despair because I see I am far from reality, and that by making myself so special I have missed out on life. Because of this I might get down on myself so much that I cling to another person to keep from drowning in self-pity. Thereby I would lose my natural spirit of independence, while drawing the other into the morass of my self-pity. As such I become very susceptible to the kind of despair that leads to suicide.

179

14. INTELLECTUAL CONVERSION[1]

According to enneagram theory, instinctual conversion involves *ascesis,* a self-discipline or effort on my part to act against my prevailing compulsion in order to overcome it and live as a more balanced personality. It concerns stretching myself to another mode of behavior by taking on the pride of another type, and letting go of the pride which was driving my compulsion. This, of course, is not sufficient for me to become whole as a person, since it does not deal directly with that which caused my ego-consciousness, which, in turn, caused me to have a compulsed personality. The strategy of moving against the arrow for instinctual conversion is like going on a diet without dealing with the cause of having an excessive hunger for food. My unsatisfied *craving* for self-fulfillment is an effect of my ego-consciousness.

Ego-consciousness is my awareness of having a split between myself and the world. Because of the fall from society, wherein I lost trust in outside reality as being conducive to my fulfillment, I am thrown on my own resources for my fulfillment. It is for this reason that I have created a defense strategy to protect the self from an alien world, and named a self-concept that limits my fulfillment to something I can attain solely by myself. From this arises my *ego-fixation,* which gets me caught in a pattern of behavior that is compulsive.

The foregoing analysis points out that the fundamental cause of my *problem* is the attitude that I am going to achieve the fulfillment of my human essence by relying

---

[1] Cf Beesing, et al., pp.156f, 178-192.

solely on my own resources. This is what we call "self-salvation."

Self-salvation

Self-salvation is a theological term. It is traditionally applied to the fifth-century doctrine of *Pelagius*, according to whom God's grace is not absolutely necessary for salvation, but is only an aid in avoiding sin. This means that solely by the power of our human will we are able avoid sin and be saved.

Self-salvation may also be applied to the naturalism of *Rousseau*, who held that the goodness of our natural instincts is such that if we follow their spontaneity they will lead us to fulfillment. According to Rousseau, what causes us to be less human all stems from the world of civilization.

Another kind of self-salvation was represented by *Nietzsche*, who taught that we can reach the fulfillment of our human potential through the use of our will to power, by which we experience the joy of conquest over obstacles.

As applied to the enneagram system, self-salvation defines the fundamental cause of my having a compulsed personality. A mistake was made in my thinking that the only fulfillment I can enjoy is that which I can attain solely by my own resources. That kind of thinking was a child's mistake, but I am tempted to keep it going out of a stance of individualism, as though denying that the fullness of being is attained only by participating in universal communion.

If I continue in the attitude of self-salvation as justified by a culture of individualism, I will simply use the enneagram for personal enhancement as another program of self-help. I will remain entrapped in my initial mistake of thinking I can realize myself solely through my own resources. The way out of this entrapment is a "leap of faith," an act of trust that outside reality is indeed friendly and beneficient toward my deepest needs and wants. In the enneagram system, this act of trust occurs by moving from a specific "trap" to a corresponding "holy idea."

Traps

The term "trap" within the enneagram system refers to an habitual way of acting derived from ego-consciousness. The trap involves getting caught in a pattern of behavior that is compulsive. This is due to my commitment to a limited value for my fulfillment, instead of dedicating myself to an unlimited or absolute value.

Each enneagram type has a specific trap, as follows: (1) perfection, (2) service, (3) efficiency, (4) authenticity, (5) knowledge, (6) security, (7) idealism, (8) justice, and (9) self-abasement. The way out of my own trap is to take on the holy idea specific to my enneagram type.

Holy Ideas

In the enneagram system, a "holy idea" is a way of relying unconditionally on God in lieu of relying on my own resources. It is here that I deal directly with the fundamental cause of my compulsiveness. It is a recognition that the alternative to relying solely on my own efforts for personal fulfillment is to turn to God for fulfillment..

There is a specific holy idea for each of the nine enneagram types, namely: (1) GROWTH, (2) GRACE, (3) GOD'S WILL, (4) UNION WITH GOD, (5) DIVINE PROVIDENCE, (6) TRUST IN GOD, (7) CO-CREATION, (8) COMPASSION, and (9) UNCONDITIONAL LOVE.

The holy idea invites me to an intellectual conversion by replacing the trap. It is an intellectual conversion by reason of being opened to ultimate reality, and as such frees me from ego-fixation based on a false idea of reality, i.e., a false idea of what life is about. Each holy idea is a way of committing myself to God's rule, to God's way of establishing the Kingdom of God. This movement from specific trap to a corresponding holy idea is to be seen as a way for each personality type to submit to God. As a consequence, it sets up a *spirituality* particular to each enneagram type, where we understand "spirituality" as a way to being fulfilled through union with God.

By submitting to a specific holy idea, I take a stance of no longer living for myself, but instead I live for God according to what is called the "divine economy."[2] Acknowledging that I am a creature rather than my own creator, I submit my life to whatever is necessary to enter God's rule in Christ. This submission to God's rule is termed "abandonment to God."

Abandonment to God

"Abandonment to God" is the basic stance required for me to enter into the grace of the Kingdom of God, which "does not come with observation,"[3] but is emphatically present in our midst, and is characterized by the rule of God over our whole lives. This represents the fundamental correction needed in my attitude which originally caused my

---

[2] The divine economy is God's predetermined plan of how we are to be united with the divine life in the Christ. It is sometimes also termed the "divine dispensation" or the "divine plan." Cf Ef 1:9.

[3] Lk 17:20

"fall from society." Instead of relying on my own autonomous resources for attaining fulfillment, by abandonment to
God I re-orientate myself by placing my fulfillment in the
hands of God.

Jesus stated that he came to give us life, "life in
abundance."[4] Divine abandonment is the key to receiving
that abundant new life. Divine abandonment occasions
both a *healing* of what distorts my being, and a being *re-
newed* with new enlightenment, new feelings, and new energy from a transcendent Source which I tap into as present
within my being.

This means that ultimately I cannot find fulfillment solely in and through myself. I am to be ultimately
fulfilled by the unlimited good that is God. It is for this
divine fulfillment that I was created and destined, but I will
never know and enjoy the divine holy mystery without becoming involved in a personal relationship with God. In
gospel terms it means no longer living for myself or seeking
to save myself, but losing my personal autonomy in order to
find myself in God's hands.[5] Following Jesus' admonition,
we lose ourselves in order to find ourselves.[6] In the terms
of St. Paul, it is casting off our old self and becoming a new
creation,[7] or allowing our outer nature to decay and our
inner nature to become new.[8]

Having gone through this introduction to intellectual conversion which is wrought by passing from traps to

---

[4] Jn 10:10
[5] Mk 8:34
[6] Mt 16:25
[7] 2 Cor 5:17
[8] 2 Cor 4:16

185

holy ideas, we are now ready to consider the spirituality particular to each enneagram type.

ONE: Perfection—>GROWTH

As a One, my trap was my idea of *perfection*. This was the false idea that reality should not be incomplete or have anything out of order. Because of this fantastic idea of perfection, I became angry when I perceived myself or the outer world as incomplete or having something out of place. For me to feel fulfilled, I needed perfection in the here and now. I pro-acted aggressively to put into reality the perfection I saw lacking.

I can let go of this unholy addiction to perfection by taking on the holy idea of GROWTH. Jesus proclaimed that God's reign comes about through a gradual growth symbolized by the development of seeds planted in a field.[9] The farmer is to tolerate the weeds that spring up in the midst of a crop, since to try to uproot them will endanger the crop itself. It is only at harvest time that the wise farmer separates the weeds from the grain.

Just as this tolerance of imperfection is needed by the farmer, so in the fostering of God's Kingdom I need to put my attention on the good that is present rather than on what is lacking. God brings about the Kingdom by a process of development. Instead of being angry about what is missing, by the holy idea of Growth I accept with satisfaction whatever good is now present. Sometimes this good is present in nothing more than seed form, but nevertheless the whole harvest is already contained in those small seeds. It is precisely by my affirming whatever is already good that I can help it to grow and develop.

---

[9] Mt 13:24-30

As a One, I am invited to share wholeheartedly the way God draws created reality into the divine Kingdom. I am to give up my outlandish notion that reality should be complete and perfect right now, and instead affirm whatever good is present as having potential for becoming more. This begins in me by accepting myself as radically good, since "God does not make junk!" It continues by affirming that I am growing through my mistakes and shortcomings, for "I am not done yet." I need to acknowledge that God rules the world in an evolutionary way.

A classic gospel text of this attitude of mistake-making as leading to greater goodness is Jesus' declaration that the sinful woman ministering to him in Simon's house shows so much love because she has had so many sins forgiven, and that "he to whom little is forgiven, loves little."[10] St. Paul also expressed the idea that we grow through our moral mistakes, saying that "however great the number of sins committed, grace was even greater."[11] Wrongdoing leads to my fulfillment because of the special graces I receive through the recognition that I am a sinner. St. Paul further says, however, that this does not mean I am to go on sinning so that grace may more abound![12] Much more will be said about grace as we go on now to take up the holy idea specific to the Two.

TWO: Service—>GRACE

The biggest mistake I made as a Two was to think I could win the love of another by my *service*. I was trapped by my idea that I would be fulfilled simply by serv-

---

[10] Lk 7:47
[11] Rm 5:20
[12] Rm 6:1

ing another. It really was a subtle form of buying love. In my pride I thought my ideal of service made me better than others. I thought my helpfulness was a great virtue, despite the fact that I needed others to be in need of me.

The holy idea of GRACE can free me from the trap of service. The term "grace" signifies gift, and in particular a gift that is undeserved. That gift which is undeserved is love. Because being loved comes from the free decision of another, true love is *undeserved*. If I am truly loved, this is because of who I am and not because of what I have done. To accept love as grace is to acknowledge that when another loves me, I am beholding an undeserved gift.

The holy idea of grace pertains to God's love for me. It is "grace" because it is an undeserved gift. God has made a free decision to love me. This love is unconditional, for God's decision to love me is not dependent on my being good. God loves me because of who I am, not because I am good. I have not earned God's love. As St. John states, God has loved us first.[13] I discover I am loved by an initiative on God's part.

What I most need to learn as a Two is that true love is unconditional. My whole approach to winning love by service assumed that the other's appreciation of me depended on my being useful or needed. The holy idea of grace shows this to be a *trap*, precisely because all true love has its source in God. As St. John writes,

> *Everyone who loves is begotten*
> *by God and knows God. Anyone*
> *who fails to love can never have*

---

[13] 1 Jn 4:10

> *known God, because God is love.*[14]

God's love is the exemplar of all true love. Since God's love is characterized by being undeserved and unconditional, there is no true love unless it is undeserved and unconditional.

This explains the strategy of Jesus in placing on God a father-image, and calling God *abba*, the English equivalent of "daddy." The bonding of parents to their offspring readily draws them to love their child before being loved by the child. Since their love is first, it is radically undeserved by the child. They also readily love their child unconditionally, as is shown by their love for their child irrespective of the child's bad behavior toward them. To *know* God I have to experience being loved undeservedly and unconditionally. This is what it is to be evangelized: to have experienced and accepted God's unconditional love.

This love God has for me has the effect of making me good by creating in me a response. When I acknowledge that I am loved and I accept it as undeserved and unconditional, I am reconciled and bonded with God. I am made good by God's prevenient love for me because it awakens in me this kind of response which makes me justified, that is, being put in right relationship with God. I experience the Christian paradox of grace, namely, that God does not love me because I am good, but I am good because God loves me.

This may be fine theology, but how does it redeem me from the domination of my compulsion as a Two? The answer is that the only love that will ever bring about my fulfillment

---

[14] 1 Jn 4:7f

is unconditional love. Any love based on the condition that I am needed, or good for another, will never satisfy my radical longing to be loved. Simply stated, unless love is wholly a gift it is not love at all.

THREE: *Efficiency—>GOD'S WILL*

As a Three, I was trapped by my addictive idea of *efficiency*. I thought I was a good person because I achieved my goals. I put my heart on being organized in order to avoid what I perceived as the great evil of failure. It was supremely important to me as a Three that others saw me as a *success*.

For me as a Three, abandonment to God involves dedicating myself to GOD'S WILL. I am to put aside the pursuit of my own goals, and place my talents in God's hands to work for the purposes of God. As a Three, I need to respect my Creator by laying down my life as one created to achieve the glory of God, rather than to work for my own glory. I need to take on the attitude of building God's Kingdom rather than a kingdom of my own.

To accept the call to be an instrument of God for God's own glory, I come to see that I have been created to be and act in a certain place. This is to accept the implications of being a *creature,* rather than being creator of myself. Why do I have all these talents and opportunities except to serve the one who placed me here?

When I work for another, I myself have less responsibility for the success of the work than when I work for myself. Working for another means I do not own the work. Since it is not my work, I am not the one who will receive the acclaim from its success, nor be the object of ridicule should it fail. By putting my efforts to do God's goals rather than my own goals, the glory of the work will not be my own, and a failure of the work will not be my own failure. I will see, then, that by working for God, failure will not diminish the worth of my person.

Once the success of my achievements is no longer the measure of my worth as a person, I am much less threatened by *failure*. Jesus himself is a model on how to accept failure. Although he worked day and night to create followers among his fellow Galileans that they would accept him as Messiah and Son of God, by the end of his life he had only a small band of believers, like a "holy remnant." The way his earthly life ended was another failure, that of not being able to convince the religious leaders at Jerusalem of the truth about himself. He accepted those failures as God's will. As it turned out, by this Jesus revealed the paschal mystery, namely, that in God's administration of the world, success comes out of failure.

St. Paul saw the failure of Jesus, especially as shown by his crucifixion, as proclaiming the message of God's salvation, that God shows his power at work through what the world despises. God continues to work through others who fail to receive honor in this world. As Paul states:

> *God chose the weak of the world*
> *to shame the strong, and God*
> *chose the lowly and despised of*
> *the world, those who count for*
> *nothing, to reduce to nothing*
> *those who are something, so that*

> *no human being might boast be-*
> *fore God.*[15]

This is a basic message for all those seeking their own success in the eyes of others. To live and work for God's will
in Christ means to serve in God's way of not receiving glory
from others, lest we "boast before God." Moreover, God
shows his power by using failure itself to achieve his own
ends, as was done by the crucifixion of Jesus.

In our time we no longer feel the shame of being
followers of a crucified man in the way it was felt by the
first Christians when crucifixion in the Roman empire was
the supreme sign of treason. Just to be known as a followers of the crucified Nazarene was cause enough to be looked
down upon by others. This is why St. Paul describes Christians as being "the foolish of the world to shame the
wise."[16] These are reflections very pertinent for me as a
Three as I sort out what makes me feel good about myself.
Whose kingdom am I working to build? If it is God's
Kingdom, can I accept my own failures in the eyes of others
as part of the God's Plan for building up the Kingdom?

FOUR: *Authenticity—>UNION WITH GOD*

As a compulsed Four, I craved *authenticity*. I had
the fantastic idea that I could be fulfilled through my own
efforts by expressing symbolically my deepest sentiments.
Because such authenticity in fact was never attained, I always felt not quite myself, as though I was still waiting for
my real life to begin. My own efforts to attain authenticity
tended to make me theatrical and unreal. In thinking that I

---

[15] 1 Cor 1:27f
[16] 1 Cor 1:27

had to make life *dramatic,* I ended up being too much of an actor, and thus even less authentic as a person.

As a Four, I need the intellectual conversion of commitment to UNION WITH GOD. This holy idea states that fulfillment comes through making my life a journey to God. Before undertaking a journey, I need a desire and a hope to go somewhere. Without a direction, my trip will be nothing more than wandering. I am called to make my desire and hope union with God, rather than authentic expression of myself. This involves abandoning myself to however God would fashion me through my life experiences. I am to rely on God making use of all my life experiences to attain the idea God has of me as a unique gift to the world at this time in history.

In order for God to mold me as a vessel on a potter's wheel,[17] I need to attend to God's presence in my life. This I can do only by living in the present moment. Since God lives only in the eternal now, I cannot really meet God in the past or in the future, but only by involvement with God in the present. There is a divine gift in the present moment which can elicit my personal response. This is what Jean-Pierre de Causade called "the sacrament of the present moment."[18] I can experience being a unique person by the way God calls me out of myself in each moment.

Any event can be an outward sign of an inbreaking divine grace. There is no such thing as an "ordinary event," nor are there spiritual experiences in life distinct from real life experiences. Any happening can be recognized as a dramatic epiphany of the transcendent, since, as Ben-Sirach

---

[17] Jer 18:1-8

[18] Cf Jean-Pierre de Causade, S.J., *Abandonment to Divine Providence,* Image Books, NY, 1975.

states, both in creation and in history *"the Lord has created an abundance of glory, and displayed the divine greatness from the earliest times."[19]* By attending to each moment, my being is readied for a wholehearted and exciting response to whatever manifests God's presence to me in the present moment. This can be for me a whole new appreciation of being free, spontaneous, and original. It fosters a deep response in me to live a creative life, and use my creativity to transform what is outside myself.

FIVE: *Knowledge*—>DIVINE PROVIDENCE

As a Five, I was trapped into compulsive behavior because of my idea that I would be fulfilled by self-acquired *knowledge*. This knowledge concerned perception and judgment, but not necessarily the kind of knowing I could have gained through interaction with persons and events. I preferred to observe life rather than participate in it. In order to control by means of knowing, I tended to compartmentalize everything, even my personal relationships. Because I took pride in having knowledge, I sometimes looked down on others as being superficial and foolish.

I often felt driven as a Five to spend time alone in order to have the knowledge I needed in order to express myself before others. I felt I needed a storehouse of knowledge in order to be "bigger than the world," i.e., to be in control of the situation, and to avoid embarrassment. To attain this storehouse of knowledge, I had to do my own thinking. Just as Fours need to be alone to practice the expression of their sentiments before standing out before others, so as a Five I needed to be alone to do my independent thinking before interacting with others.

---

[19] Sir 44:2. Cf 42:16.

As a Five, I can be freed from my trap of knowledge through the holy idea of DIVINE PROVIDENCE. This entails my placing trust in God's promise to provide for all my needs. For me as a Five to trust divine providence will include the confidence that I will be provided with what I need to know in order to function well. This means that I let life itself become my teacher. I come to trust that whatever I will need in order to perform adequately in the public arena will be made available to me through what happens to me beforehand. It may come by way of what others say to me, what comes in the mail, or through what comes to my attention in some other way.

In order for life to be my teacher, however, I cannot remain an interested bystander. I need to become involved. I cannot be adequately in touch with divine providence simply by reading the right books, or having sufficient time for personal reflection. I am to trust that *in the action itself* the divine Spirit will prompt me in what I need to say.[20] In order to get over my former worries about performing well, I simply need to rely on God's care of me.

By such abandonment to God, I can be transformed as a Five to become a very active person, taking on a multitude of different tasks and projects. With my ability to compartmentalize my life into segments, I can move from one task to another with an inner freedom, while keeping my ear to the ground to hear from many voices what will prepare me to perform well. Without need for any more preparation than time allows, I trust that I will be led to know what to say and how to react when the moment of performance arrives. This is for me to let God be God in my life. Through my abandonment to divine providence, my

---

[20] Cf Lk 12:11f

quest to know becomes less a seeking to be left alone, and more a sharing of the heart with others on what each of us sees as significant and holds as cherished. This attitude of sharing comes from my new conviction that not to be involved is to miss the greatest reality, the holy mystery of God.

What we call "mystery" can be defined as that which can be known only by personal involvement. It may also be characterized as that of which we can always know something more. In both cases, knowing another person is indeed knowing a mystery. This leads me to appreciate the significance of sharing the inner world of others. I see that all my involvement is to lead me to personal communion, and that not to share the hearts of others is to miss reality. I also discover an inner yearning to be known as well as to know. This leads me out of my native aloofness into living much more in my heart center with its sensitivity to relationships with others. I become convinced that if I am only a great observer of life, I will really miss what is going on. Only by becoming a *participant* through personal communion will I keep from missing what is truly significant.

My self-confidence grows also from believing in myself because I believe God believes in me. I am to recognize the gifts and talents I have, and the personal resources that have been built up in my inner world through past experience and reflection. Through my communion with significant friends, I have no doubt about these inner gifts and my own goodness, and so I am able to confront adversaries with a conviction that I have great personal strength and the support of friends who believe in me.

SIX: Security—>TRUST IN GOD

As a Six, I was trapped by my preoccupation with *security*. Unlike a Five, I looked outside myself for my security, rather than inside myself. I saw my fulfillment in the security given me by conforming to social norms and authorities. I was convinced that loyalty to a leader was a solution to the problem of my prevailing indecision and self-doubt.

If I held a position of authority, I governed others mainly by regulations handed down to me. Sometimes what I considered to be my own decisiveness was in reality authoritarianism. I tended to consider any questioning of my own ideas and procedures as a personal attack. Because I identified myself emotionally with the group or institution to which I belonged, I considered as personal enemies or antagonists all those who defied my group or institution.

I can be freed from my trap of security as a Six by the holy idea of TRUST IN GOD. I need to see that trust in human authorities and regulations can never simply substitute for direct trust in God. Here, though, I need to see God not as lawgiver, but as filled with parental love for me. As long as I believe that security comes from loyalty to outside authority, I will tend to project upon God the image of a lawgiver and judge. It is only by taking to heart the gospel message of divine adoption that as a Six I can be freed from my trap. Only then does God cease to be a threat to my security, and become a refuge even when I have failed God by my sins.

The gospel message of divine adoption through faith and baptism means that nothing can hurt me because God has decided to be my parent. My filial bond with God thereby precedes any external observances. I can sense how this changes the way I look at *deviance* by asking myself this questions: "To whom would I go if I broke a civil law, to a judge or to my family?" By my answer that I would go to my family, I can see how by making God a lawgiver and judge, I will always fear God rather than have faith in God. That in itself shows that my outlook as a compulsed Six got in the way of relating to God as confidante and protector.

The result of this intellectual conversion from the trap of security to the holy idea of trust in God is that as a Six I come to see that being a good person is not realized by external observances. I am primarily called to live out of who I am as child of God, rather than try to shape up to be justified in God's sight by conformity to external norms. Respect for such norms, such as the Ten Commandments, may indeed be an expression of my filial love for God, but my motive is not to escape punishment as a lawbreaker, but rather to take God as model for my own attitudes.

God does make demands of me, but what God asks of me and promises me can never be completely indicated by laws and institutions. After all, structures, customs, and laws are subject to change, but my responsibility to God as adopted child remains constant. Here I need to see morality and responsibility not primarily as obeying laws, but rather as *promoting values*. The values are seen as characteristic of divine attitudes, such as compassion, honesty, fidelity, and, above all, love itself. My very bondedness to God as adopted child means that I am responsible to take on such divine attitudes. As St. Paul states, we are to be "imitators of God as God's beloved children."[21]

Values I am to live out in my life do exist within good laws, but they are not adequately made real by external

---

[21] Eph 5:1

observances. If it is not mainly by obeying laws, how do I make values real in my life? It is primarily by a personal commitment to them. That is the way they are "incarnated" in me. These values are greater than I am. For that reason, I put these values in my life by being ready to sacrifice all I am for the values, just as Jesus lived and died for the truth of God which he revealed.

SEVEN: Idealism—>CO-CREATION

As a Seven, I was trapped into compulsive behavior because of my *idealism*. I was on a head trip, thinking how nice things were. I wanted to dispel all gloom by my habitual smile. To preserve my ideal that life should be cheerful, I sought to avoid and deny whatever was painful. Since my experience in the present often was not this ideal, I tended to compensate by planning ahead to make happen what would be exciting. Whenever carrying out one of my plans proved to be painful in some way, I would not stick with it. Such procrastination and failure in my commitments could be very troublesome to others. As a compulsed Seven, I did not really want to hurt anyone, and so I responded with an optimistic air of pleasantries to complaints from others that I did not follow through with what I had said I would do.

To me as a Seven, anything could be interesting, especially if I could talk about it. I expected others to see me as always very nice, even if they experienced me as superficial and undependable. I needed to recognize that even though I thought my idealism made me a good person radiating cheerfulness, others did not always experience me as being that helpful as a person. I would disappoint my friends, not only by my procrastination, but also by running away from intimacy.

By the holy idea of CO-CREATION, I can be freed as a Seven from my trap of idealism, and find fulfillment in abandonment to God. Co-creation is to work with God, the Creator, in the betterment of creation. In this, however, I am committed to work according to God's Plan, and that means I have to accept pain and privations as the necessary price to be paid to bring about good. It is fundamental to the gospel message that any holy work must include the cross, because according to the gospel message creation is to be restored through the passion, death, and resurrection of Jesus. This is what is called "the paschal mystery."

The gospel gives great value to suffering. Even though suffering is an evil, it is the necessary pathway for achieving any good of lasting value. It is not that we seek suffering, but we are willing to suffer for what we want to achieve, and in making plans we expect that we will have to pay a price of pain for their fulfillment. This includes the details of work, and the daily grind of patient service to others. Jesus compared such acceptance of pain as akin to the suffering of childbirth. When the labor pains begin the mother is sad, but once the child is born she forgets what she has gone through because of the joy that a child has come into the world.[22]

As a compulsed Seven, I saw pain as a pure negation of life. Now I see that in accepting to work with Jesus to bring about life in abundance, I must accept to carry my daily cross behind him.[23] Jesus carried his cross to transform this world into God's Kingdom. Unless I do it his way by carrying my cross behind him, I cannot be sure that I am engaged in God's work for the Kingdom.

---

[22] Jn 16:20-22
[23] Cf Lk 9:23

EIGHT: Justice—>COMPASSION

As a Eight, I was trapped into compulsive behavior because of my extravagant idea of *justice*, whereby I thought I was the arbiter of right and wrong. I thought it was my position to decide what is just and what is unjust, and I liked to confront whatever I saw as wrong in the world. To prove my own strength always seemed good to me, even if it was at the expense of others. I enjoyed any confrontation which would test the strength of my personality, and I liked to clear the air by having it out with others. When others annoyed or contradicted me, I felt it right that I should make them suffer for it.

The way out of my trap of justice is by my abandonment to God's holy idea of COMPASSION. To imitate the perfection of God, I am to be compassionate as my heavenly Father is compassionate.[24] In the face of human weakness, God responds with tenderness rather than harshness. Since I have tended to despise *weakness*, taking on the idea of compassion is going to change my personality. The tenderness of compassion is like that of being a parent or sibling of someone in misfortune, wherein I am with him or her, and I do what I can to be of comfort.

Moving from justice to divine compassion also means I am to avoid vengeance. Instead of seeking retribution, I am to do good to those who do evil to me. God's justice is not to chastise for wrongs done, but rather it consists in tolerance, non-violence, patience, and forgiveness. This is how God rules by justice. If we doubt that because of the idea we have of God as chastiser, we need to turn to Jesus. His attitudes were very different from that of a chastiser as he hung from the cross and said, "Father, forgive

---

[24] Lk 6:32-37

201

them for they know not what they do."[25]   Jesus is the perfect revelation of how God is. Jesus said that those who saw him saw the heavenly Father.[26]

If I, then, as an Eight would hear the gospel and take on its teaching, I must put aside all arrogance and all revenge. Even, and especially, to enemies,—to those who cause me pain or fear,—I am to direct a heartfelt love and forgiveness. Unless indeed I love my enemies, doing good to those who do harm to me, I have not even taken the first step in loving my neighbor according to the message of Jesus, since it is by that in particular that I show I am a child of God. As Jesus says, "love your enemies, and pray for those who persecute you, that you may be children of your heavenly Father."[27]

It is here that as an Eight I need to consider what is called "the power of martyrdom."[28]   Too often Christians have thought romantically of martyrdom as a "ticket to heaven," like the attitude of the eight-year-old Teresa of Avila, as described in the first chapter of her *Life*. She led her older brother, Rodrigo, to try to run away from home so they would be beheaded by the Moors "in order," as she says, "to attain as quickly as possible the fruition of the great blessings (of heaven)." Actually, however, the call to martyrdom as addressed to Christians points to the power martyrdom has to convert our persecutors. By my patient and non-violent response toward those who oppress me,

---

[25] Lk 23:34

[26] Jn 14:9

[27] Mt 5:44f

[28] I have developed the notion of martyrdom in relation to the Eight more extensively in *Nine Portraits of Jesus*, pp. 107-112.

rather than by responding in kind to their violence against me, I bear *witness* to the justice and truth of my cause. On the other hand, should I defend myself in a violent way by doing injury to my opponents, they will feel justified in overcoming me by violence, and be less likely to feel remorse. As Jesus indicates, it is by our suffering unjust persecution with patience that the Holy Spirit has the power to convince the world of its injustice.[29]

NINE: *Self-abasement*—>UNCONDITIONAL LOVE

My basic problem as a Nine was that I had been putting myself down, and feeling okay in doing just that. This trap of *self-abasement* had brought about my compulsive behavior of ego-indolence. I had been convinced that I was not very attractive or interesting as a person, and so I was content with doing little and expecting little from life. I contented myself with puttering around, and leaving it up to others to initiate activity.

It may not have been news to me that I needed love, but I did need to hear the *good news* that I am invited as a Nine to submit myself to the holy idea of UNCONDITIONAL LOVE. This means that I accept that God loves me because of who I am. I am to believe that in God's eyes I am very lovable, and have always been very lovable.

At a certain time in history, God looked at the world and said he needed me there, with the gift of my special talents and goodness. This is why I was born when and where and as I was. I was God's gift to the world because I was what the world needed as God saw the situation.

---

[29] Cf Jn 16:8-11

After making me, God threw away the model. No one else will ever exist or has ever existed with exactly the same gifts that I have. I am a unique gift from God to the world. God has loved me into existence as a special edition of divine image and likeness, and particularly suited for what people need at this time. As God continues to address the world with good news, I am a word of that good news because of the gifts and talents I have.

To be that good news from God, however, I must esteem myself, for God cannot give a negative gift. God loves me for the gift I am, and loves others by placing me among them as a gift from God to them.

Having been drawn into the conviction that if God has loved me so deeply and unconditionally, I have an incentive to show that same love for others.[30] By bearing in mind that God out of love has taken a initiative to make me a gift to this world, I, in turn, will want to make myself a positive gift to others. I will see that love takes initiative, and so in presenting myself to others I will seek to do that which is best for them. This will help me considerably in having the energy to be outgoing and enterprising in how I can make others feel good about themselves however they are. I will also want to know better my gifts and take pains to develop that which will truly benefit others.

---

[30] Cf 1 Jn 4:11

15. AFFECTIVE CONVERSION[1]

Because I was created and destined for God, I have in my being a spontaneous yearning for God which can find its satisfaction and peace only in the divine mystery. By having chosen a false sense of reality as represented by my ego-fixation, I suffer a chronic distortion in my spontaneous yearning for God, because something less than God has been chosen as my unlimited, definitive good. My yearning for God, as represented by my passionate love, becomes distorted in what is called a *passion*. The response of passionate love to a false sense of reality sets up a *craving*, because a love for the unlimited good of God can never be fully satisfied by what is limited. Even in attaining the goal I have set up as my fulfillment, I will still crave for more. I never will be completely satisfied.

As we have seen, abandonment to God involves an intellectual conversion of taking on a specific holy idea to replace the trap of my compulsion. This can lead to a further conversion called "affective conversion," which heals the distortion of my passionate love caused by fixing as my ultimate fulfillment some good which is limited and attainable solely by my own efforts. Since the chosen self-fulfillment differs with each enneagram type, the distortion of the passionate love also will differ with each type. The distortion of each type's passionate love is designated as a passion specific to that type. Each passion results from the response of love being distorted by a false sense of reality.

As a distortion of my passionate love, my specific passion constitutes a *vice*. It disposes me to a false fulfill-

---

[1] Cf Beesing, et al., pp. 120-134, 193-199, 210-218.

205

ment, and sets up my life for continued frustration, because of a false hope coming out of self-deception. By my ego-fixation, I have directed myself down a certain path toward self-fulfillment, and the bias of a false sense of reality makes it difficult for me to recognize that I have a problem. My false sense of reality has set up a distortion in my own conscience. As a result of this blindness or bias regarding virtue and vice, in living out of my ego-fixation I am going to resist recognizing my specific passion. I will consider that fault, or vice, as actually my supreme virtue. This stiffens my resistance against changing my dispositions, and keeps me from being remorseful about what is in reality a vice.

The passion, then, is a strong disposition of my affective nature stimulated by what I hold as good in my heart. Even though I have already straightened out my sense of reality, and chosen abandonment to God as my goal in life for my fulfillment, there is still need for considering the specific passion that I have been used to in my affective life. The passion needs to be healed, and the healing of it occurs through a permanent disposition of my soul called a virtue. The virtue specific to each enneagram type is a permanent disposition which expresses in a specific way one's love for God as absolute good.

This healing of the specific passion by the specific virtue is called "affective conversion." It follows from the new spiritual track set up by abandonment to God, but nonetheless it involves my deliberately choosing to live according to the virtue replacing the passion.

Following around the enneagram points, then, in affective conversion we move from passion to virtue as follows: (1) from anger to *serenity*, (2) from pride to *humility*, (3) from deceit to *truthfulness*, (4) from envy to *equanimity*,

(5) from stinginess to *detachment,* (6) from fear to *courage,* (7) from over-indulgence to *sobriety,* (8) from arrogance to *simplicity,* and (9) from laziness to *diligence.*

Totems

We will conclude our consideration of each type with mention of its totems. We know totems from the religious heritage of Native Americans. Totems connote a kinship between one's personality and a certain subhuman living creature. In the enneagram system we move from one totem to another as we are healed of our compulsion and become a *redeemed* type, with our personality freed from the domination of its characteristic compulsion. It is especially in our affective life that we identify with our particular totem, whether out of our specific passion as a compulsed type, or out of our specific virtue as a redeemed type.

Redemption.

It is appropriate to use the term "redeemed" to designate a type which has overcome its compulsion by a conversion. The term "redemption" implies paying a price to release captives. As applied to the enneagram system, redemption is paying the price necessary to overcome our compulsion. It is "paying a price" because overcoming a compulsion involves actions contrary to our inclinations. On the deepest level, as we have seen, this means leaving aside our attitude of self-salvation, and abandoning ourselves to be ruled by God. Christians believe that even God paid a price that we be made able to participate in the divine mystery.

The Serene One

Anger—>Serenity

As a compulsed One, I suffered from my passion of anger, the _attitude of being dissatisfied because things were not the way I wanted them to be._ This anger was engendered by addiction to the fantastic idea that both I and others should be perfect right now. This fussiness and critical attitude on my part caused others often not to feel at home with me, as though being correct was more important to me than our getting along together. My anger was often turned against myself through the voice of my inner critic. This voice interrupted the flow of my thoughts to get me to check up on myself. It also was readily projected on others with an exacting attitude.

The abandonment I have made to God's rule through the holy idea of GROWTH not only releases me from the trap of perfection; it also can heal me of my passion of anger. I come to see the wisdom of fostering whatever I see of good, and drawing out of people their capacities for growth. At the same time, I sense that the spontaneous movements of my inner nature are much more worthy of my trust than I thought in the past. As I befriend my inner appetites and yearnings, I come to see that my feelings are me, and I need to value them. I come to sense that especially the expression of affection has a healing power over all my emotions. In this way, my passionate love is channeled towards that which is good, so that my anger is gradually replaced by the virtue of _serenity_, enabling my soul to have a permanent disposition of self-composure.

*Terrier—>*ANT

As a compulsed One, I was identified with my totem of the *terrier*. I "snapped at heels" by my critical stance of *shoulds*. I intervened too much in the lives of others, at least by my thoughts. People tended to be afraid of me because I might find something wrong with them, and be strict with them about it.

By my affective conversion to *serenity*, I can now identify more with my new totem of the ANT. Ants mind their own business as they keep constantly at work. Like an ant I serenely go about carrying out what for me are enormous tasks. I work in conjunction with others, but without interfering in what they are doing or how they are.

The Humble Two

*Pride—>*Humility

As a compulsed Two, my dominant passion was *pride*. Because I avoided having any needs, others were not allowed to do anything for me. This gave me an air of independence, and in effect told them I was not needy. I thought the avoidance of having needs made me selfless, but actually it expressed pride because I was denying I needed others for my own welfare. At the same time, however, I was fishing for appreciation from others, and trying to make them dependent on service that only I could give them.

Through taking on the holy idea of GRACE, I have learned that I need to be loved for myself, rather than for my service. Since the satisfaction of this need to be loved for my own sake is not something I can earn from others by doing something for them, I end up always in need, and that disposition can be called *humility*. My need to be loved may call out from another a response of being fond of me, but that is not something I can earn on my own, or ever be sure of getting simply by being myself.

Such radical neediness inclines me to tears of gratitude when I do receive the gift of love. I respond by casting aside all the strategies of flattery, and concentrate on sharing myself. Having come to like myself by the discovery of God's being fond of me because of who I am, and not because I have done something to win God's favor, I am more willing to be known as I truly am. I am also freed to express great fondness for others without performing services for them, or showering them with gifts.

Cat—>IRISH SETTER

Because of my pride as a compulsed Two, my totem was the *cat*. Like a cat I would express affection for another, and then march off with an air of independence. I would try to control my relationships by manipulating others to appreciate me.

My acceptance of the holy idea of GRACE has disposed my affective life to feel neediness of others, since I now see that the love I want from others is not something I can win by service, but rather is a gift they decide to give me. Another will decide to give me that gift of love by knowing me as I really am. For this reason I have to disclose my heart. Whatever love others give me, I receive gratefully because I see it as undeserved, while at the same time truly needed by me in order that I be a good person. By another's sheer goodness, that person loves goodness into me.

For this reason, my redeemed totem is the IRISH SETTER, which is characterized by intimacy as well as effusiveness. Having come to like myself by the discovery of God's favor toward me because of who I am, and not because of something I have done for God, I in turn will love the persons in my life without putting them in debt to my service.

The Magnanimous Three

Deceit—>Truthfulness

My craving for success as a Three was really vanity. It was a matter of the image I created before others. This, then, resulted in my having a passion of *deceit*. What I was yearning for was not really achievements, but rather *appearances*. Hence, in my competitiveness and my manner of presenting myself before others, I was boastful. I tended to exaggerate my success, or I would seek to sell others on what I was promoting by putting on a false sincerity. In the final analysis, since success was my fulfillment, I tended to make that end as justification for whatever means I used to attain it.

Having abandoned myself to God's rule in my life through the holy idea of GOD'S WILL, I now recognize that God's Kingdom is based on truth. As Jesus said to the ambitious Pilate:

> *"I was born and came into this world to be a witness of truth. Anyone committed to the truth hears my voice"*[2]

---

[2] Jn 18:37

In dedicating myself to building God's Kingdom, I know I need integrity. Instead of conspiring to take advantage of others and get ahead of them, I am called upon to be sincere and open with others in personal disclosure. Only in this way can I build up trust among individuals and groups, so that people are bonded together in mutual love and collaboration.

This outlook on my work undertaken for God also moderates the craving I had for one success after another. When I identified success with my worth, I could never have enough, because no one success satisfied the yearning I had for unlimited worth. Now that I see my worth in terms of doing God's will, I simply want to be where God wants me to be as a servant doing what God wants me to do.

*Peacock—>*BALD EAGLE

As a compulsed Three, I was given as my totem the *peacock,* which struts in front of others to get their attention. I had to get a favorable attention from others in order to feel esteemed because of my achievements. Now I see that this was simply *vanity.*

By giving myself over to promoting God's will on earth for the coming of the Kingdom of God, I take on as a Three the new totem of the BALD EAGLE. Instead of misusing my courage and resolution for the sake of vainglory, as a redeemed Three I express a lofty spirit of sacrifice for a good greater than myself, the common good of humankind. I feel good about having a magnanimous spirit, putting to work my talents and courage generously for the better ordering of human society.[3] I really am a big-hearted person.

---

[3] Cf Vatican II, *Gaudium et Spes,* 39.

The Free-spirited Four

Envy—>Equanimity

Since my friends saw me as a very cultured person as a Four, they were often surprised that I was envious when someone else stood out as a person of good taste. Perhaps they simply attributed it to my "artistic temperament," but in actuality *envy* was my dominant passion. That was because I found my worth in being special and unique. Since this was an unlimited craving, it was competitive. For me to feel good about myself, I needed to draw attention to myself in my unique refinement, and not have another steal the limelight from me. I was, after all, very "self-absorbed."

My abandonment to the holy idea of UNION WITH GOD, by seeking above all to respond to the presence of God in the present moment, can free me from this envy, such that I live on a deeper level of my being, freed from my former preoccupations which caused self-absorption. By seeking to let God's presence draw out from me a free response in the now-moment, I find myself naturally growing in the self-composure called *equanimity*. Even when I am under stress, I am able to "let go and let God," and thereby relax in the enjoyment of beauty all around me.

Since I cannot fully anticipate what the next moment will be, my life will be full of surprises, and thereby call out from me a spectrum of emotions. These emotions are not necessarily programmed from past hurts, but may be ever new in the expression of myself. I am stretched as a free spirit, caught up in the mystery of life as lived moment by moment. I cannot know how I will be in the future, because my life is lived by responses to situations as they occur. All the while, I am yearning to meet the beauty of divine presence seen in its fullness.

*Basset Hound—>*BLACK STALLION

Inasmuch as I enjoyed pining in the melancholy of sweet regrets about my past tragic experiences, my totem as a compulsed Four was the *basset hound.* Moodiness and being super-sensitive about small hurts placed me in a certain isolation from others, and my feeling of being misunderstood only added to my ego-fixation of melancholy.

Having now placed the fulfillment of my life in the hands of God by reason of my intellectual conversion, I feel myself to be gifted with the new totem of the BLACK STALLION. This represents my free spirit and graceful self-possession, as I readily respond gracefully to the gift of the present moment. I delight in the beauty of being free-spirited, and am deeply grateful for being a unique creature of God set in the midst of all God's works.

The Detached Five

*Stinginess—>*Detachment

As a compulsed Five, I justified my passion of stinginess, because holding on to my resources gave me the good feeling of security. I paid little attention to what others might be saying about my personality. Being a very independent person, as long as I thought I was okay, I concluded I was okay. I kept busy attending to my inner world, as that which was most interesting in my life. I was noted for clinging to my time, my space, and my privacy. In this way I kept control of my life.

Now that I have handed over my life to God through the idea of DIVINE PROVIDENCE, being "out of control" and in God's care is becoming more my stance for a secure life. I want to feel that I am not living my own schedule, as much as a divine schedule of events in which I am a participant and a beneficiary. Instead of storing up resources for future action, I try to live off the gifts of the day. In this way, the virtue of *detachment* is healing my passion of stinginess.

Fox—>OWL

As a compulsed Five, my totem of the *fox* was symptomatic of my compulsion to observe from a protective aloofness because of fear of being drawn into dangerous situations. It also pointed to my quest for privacy in my own den, where my activity was hidden from the knowledge of others, even from my closest friends.

Now that my intellectual conversion to the holy idea of divine providence has given me a new security in God's providing me what I need for activities, I appreciate identifying with my new totem of the OWL. Like the owl, I now feel secure that I will have whatever resources I will need for doing whatever work I am to do. I know I have the ability not only to know what to do, but also the power to achieve it in action. Should I be opposed by others in an unjust way, I will know how to draw on skills to counter them effectively. I have this self-confidence in my own ability, because I know God is my partner not only in my reflection, but also, and especially, in my action.

The Courageous Six

Fear—>Courage

Because of my trap of security as a compulsed Six, my dominant passion was *fear*. I doubted my own judgment so much that I was often apprehensive lest I make a mistake. I experienced life as very threatening. Often I anguished over making a decision, all the time realizing that not to decide was to decide. That, too, made me very anxious.

Abandonment to God through trust because of my divine adoption has freed me from much of my former fear of making mistakes. Knowing that nothing can separate me from God's parental love, I can try out new ways to promote values in society, even though these are not mandated by an outside authority. This new stance of relying on God's parental love for me as that which puts me in right relationship with God gives me a *courage* to do new things on my own, and to make decisions in matters that are tentative and risky, without going through an agony of self-doubt. I can also accept changes much more readily, since I have given up thinking that what assures my security is conformity to outside norms and customs. Since no personality type has struggled with fear as much as my type, it is understandable that for me as a Six to conquer fear will make *courage* my outstanding virtue.

Rabbit—>DEER

As a compulsed Six, I lived out the totem of the *rabbit*. I lived with nervous apprehension, lest by lowering my guard I should fall into danger. I tended to react to danger by panic behavior, instead of directly facing with assurance whatever threatened me.

Having come to live now in trust of God, I have been given the new totem of the DEER. I have grown in a relaxed alertness to any possible dangers, for I know that I will be able to escape any calamity with calmness and self-composure. I know I have grown quite fearless after having come to recognize that the fear in myself was the main enemy I needed to overcome. Like a deer, I avoid facing life alone. I have learned to share closely with others my joys, sorrows, and dangers. This sharing itself is a big part of feeling secure.

The Earnest Seven

Over-indulgence—>Sobriety

As a compulsed Seven, my dominant passion was *over-indulgence*. Since pleasure produced a sensation of good cheer, in seeking cheerfulness in life I tended to seek pleasure for its own sake. This easily led to over-indulgence, especially because my craving for fulfillment by cheerfulness created a need in me to have one cheerful happening after another, or to prolong the good time I was having at the moment.

Having now accepted my mission in life as working for God under the divine plan for CO-CREATION, I am growing as a Seven in the virtue of *sobriety*. I am becoming more *earnest* by bearing whatever pain is necessary to give birth to my dreams. I seek solitude for study and reflection as a way of living out this greater seriousness. It seems to me that God is calling me to be willing to suffer for some great cause, and my being alone with myself and God does aid me in being more ready to respond, so that with dogged determination I complete what I have set out to do to make life better for others. I have come to recognize that the worth of my life indeed does depend a lot of hard work.

Monkey—>BUTTERFLY

As a compulsed Seven, I had to admit that the *monkey* totem did fit me well. I was something of a "swinger." I liked to mimic, to amuse, and to be excitedly up in the air. It seems I was ever chattering and on the move. I particularly enjoyed having a lot of like-minded people around me to keep up the excitement.

Now as a redeemed Seven abandoned to God's ways, I have been given a new totem, the BUTTERFLY. My new personality has emerged after a long period of darkness involving loss and grief, all of which has made me much more serious about working for God. Like a butterfly, I seek to reflect the sunshine of life, but at the same time I accept that goodness and joy often comes out of much pain. I also must face the shortness of life in this world, and make the best of my limited time to keep in touch with many persons, in order to give them support and encouragement, and to work with them to create a better life for many.

The Childlike Eight

Arrogance—>Simplicity

I do not like to admit that as a compulsed Eight I had an arrogant streak, and that in fact my predominant passion was *arrogance* itself. I did not like to put myself down as though I had some glaring defect of personality. It was true, of course, that I tended to push others around, especially those that were a push-over. I thought at the time that their weakness was their own problem.

Now, however, having accepted the holy idea of COMPASSION as the way to abandon myself to God's rule of my life, I am discovering in myself what can be called the virtue of *simplicity*. I guess I always was childlike in my own heart, and my tendency to be aggressive stemmed from an inner insecurity. I thought I had to be strong in order to defend myself, and make others respect me.

In grappling with my own character, I am reminded of Louis Burbank trying to create a species of rose
without thorns. Finally he knelt down before a rose plant
and begged it not to be afraid to lose its thorns. I think I
have been like that rose plant, and others around me have
been begging me not to be afraid anymore, that I feel more
secure with social reality, and become less suspicious and
cynical. I know for me to take that direction in my attitude
would be to awaken the inner child in me, that child who in
the past was hurt by a strong authority figure.

I am invited to accept people as they are, with a
mixture of virtue and vice, good motives and bad, along
with their other strengths and weaknesses. As I recognize
that I can love and trust others who have weak points and
even dark secrets, I will be more ready and able to befriend
my own shadowy parts and accept all the opposites and
contradictions within myself as complementary and thereby
conducive to my wholeness as a person. Having come to
know and befriend my weak side, I can live in greater inner
security. This can tame my aggressive nature, which developed out of fear and anxiety. Feeling much less under attack from others, I can be more content to live in friendship,
rather than have to assert my independence in order to feel
good about myself.

Rhinoceros—>TIGER

In my arrogance as a compulsed Eight, I was identified with the totem of the thick-skinned *rhinoceros*. I had
to keep on my armor because to me life was a warfare, and
opponents might attack me unexpectedly from any quarter.
I felt that the best defense was offense, and so I would
automatically try to topple over whatever I thought was
dangerous to me.

Now that I have abandoned myself to the holy idea of compassion, I have been given a new totem: the TIGER. I now know I am strong without feeling I have to prove it by confronting and testing others. I express my playful and affectionate side to family and friends, and reserve my great strength only when others need my help, whether because they cannot lift themselves out of misery, or because they are unable to defend themselves from oppression.

The Industrious Nine

Laziness—>**Diligence**

As a compulsed Nine, my dominant passion was *laziness,* because I wanted to be content with life as I found it. My contentment would be upset by tension, conflict, and strong feelings, so I backed away from those experiences. I developed an attitude of taking things easy. I chided my friends and associates for always running around and working too hard. I thought that even Almighty God was easy-going. Underlying this, of course, was the experience of not feeling important to others early in my life, and adjusting myself to be of no trouble to them.

In my intellectual conversion to the holy idea of UNCONDITIONAL LOVE, I have had a great change in the way I look at myself. I have begun to see that God has placed me in this world as someone very precious and unique. This has caused me to want to know better what my gifts are, and to set about developing my potential. Whereas before I was content to amuse myself and others with pastimes, now I want to set some goals for myself, and to work at them step by step. I am putting my nose to the grindstone as a patient, methodical worker, day by day, year in and year out. My old passion of laziness is being healed by the virtue of *diligence*. I have changed from being a putterer to being a *plodder*. I get the job done because I keep at it. After all, I know I have a *destiny*.

Elephant—>PORPOISE

When I was compulsed as a Nine, I had the totem of the *elephant*. I was a ponderous, but easy-going person. Others found it hard to move me, and often they had to work around me. I had big ears, but sometimes I failed to understand what others were saying, or just did not want to understand.

Now, however, as a redeemed Nine through accepting the holy idea of unconditional love, I have been given a new totem: the PORPOISE. Like a porpoise I have a lot of energy. I do not withdraw from others like I used to do, but am fond of living and working alongside others in community. I look out for others, and am very friendly to everyone as their brother or sister. I am a very good community person.

Epilogue

In the sacred scriptures, the quest for personal transformation through union with God is often symbolized as climbing a mountain.[1] Moses climbed Mount Sinai, met God, and as a transformed person came back down the mountain to complete his life work. Many centuries later, the prophet Elijah climbed that same mountain, encountered God, and came down the mountain to complete his life work. Jesus himself climbed a very high mountain with three disciples, was transfigured in a vision of glory, and came down the mountain to complete his life work.

Not everyone cares to try to climb a mountain, just as not everyone cares to seek God. There has to be a yearning. The yearning for union with God arises out of some dissatisfaction with my life, from an emptiness in my heart.

As I look back in my life, however, I may remember a time when I did not yearn for God. My heart was not empty. It was full,—full of myself. On the throne of my heart, I had placed ME. Perhaps I had a habit of sin, which I confessed but did not change. I found religion full of commandments and other obligations which got in the way of my enjoying life. I may have sought pleasure even at the expense of others, and fled from the feeling of being alone by all kinds of noise. Maybe I just wanted to make a lot of money. Mayhap I wished that God did not exist, so I could do whatever I wanted, or I began to doubt that there was a God.

---

[1] Cf Is 2:2f; Mi 4:1ff.

Because of something that happened in my life, I decided to take ME off the throne. Something happened to make me dissatisfied with myself, with my companions, or with life itself. There was an emptiness in my heart that caused me to look to a Higher Power. Maybe I noticed others as happy, and I wasn't happy. Maybe I was attracted to someone who was very generous, and then I saw how mean and selfish I was. Perhaps I recognized I was in the pit of a serious addiction, and was unable to climb out by myself. Maybe I was just very lonely.

Taking ME off the throne of my heart was like being persuaded to climb a high mountain for the first time. I set out in the early morning with my companions, and began following a well-marked path through the woods. Following the signs represented the fact that to find God, I had to put order in my life by doing God's will as clearly shown by the commandments and the laws of the Church. I had to recognize that God had rights over me. In the past, I had failed in my obligations toward God. Now I resolved to listen to my conscience. Remembering a debt I had not paid, I put the money in an envelope and sent it in the mail. I had been using people. Now I saw they had the same rights as I. I resolved to turn away from temptations, and be sincere in my prayers. I took on a life of *duty*. On the throne of my heart, I placed God's LAW.[2] .

After walking on the path for a long while, I stopped to rest with my companions. Some other hikers come along, and asked the way to the top of the mountain. I told them to keep on the path, and just follow the signs. I really did not know much about climbing a mountain. All I

---

[2] Cf Ps 119:11-- *"I keep your law in my heart."*

had been doing was walking through the woods, but I thought that was all there was to it.

This is the way I had come to see religion: that all there is to religion is keeping the rules. I even thought prayer itself was simply the fulfillment of an obligation. I had developed an attitude of self-righteousness. I was very critical of others who did not keep the rules. As for myself, I felt justified in everything I did. I did not see I ever committed a sin. I did not really believe I was a sinner in need of salvation.

By thinking that religion was just a matter of keeping the rules, I had gotten lost in the woods. I was forgetting that I had set out to climb a mountain, and became content simply to walk through the woods on a well-marked trail. My friends, however, reminded me that we were to climb a mountain.

As I continued on the path, the signs became more and more simple. In my spiritual journey, I came to see that all the commandments were reduced to two: love God and love neighbor. Then these two were reduced to just one: if I did not love the neighbor I could see, how could I say I loved God whom I could not see?[3] I began to wonder if I loved anyone.

All of a sudden, I broke out of the woods. I was above the tree line. There was bright sunshine, a fresh, mountain breeze, and birds were singing. Ahead of me was green grass and mountain flowers, and in the distance I saw the mountaintop, which I had not been able to see in the woods. I did not need the signs anymore. I did not need

---

[3] Cf 1 Jn 4:20

the path anymore. I wasn't even tired anymore. Full of joy, I ran toward the mountaintop.

This breaking out of the woods represents what may be called a *second conversion*. For each person, it may occur in a different way. People had been reaching out to me, as though something was wrong with me, and that they wanted to help. Someone said that what I did was all right, but not the way I did it. Another person, who did not even know the first person, said the same thing, in the very same words. As I was pondering this, suddenly I saw that it was Jesus in these people who was saying these things to me.

When I saw it was Jesus, I knew what was wrong. I saw that often I was stern and irritable toward others. I had felt that I needed to correct people, to get them to shape up. Now, however, I saw that these feelings of sternness and harshness were me, and that I did not want to be that way. I wanted to be a Christian.

That I had been so blind about my faults, while others clearly saw them, showed me that I was blind about myself. I needed to be close to others so that I could see myself through their eyes. Otherwise I would continue to be blind, and live with a false idea of myself. I also saw that a reason I was irritable and unkind was that I did not feel I was loved. Maybe others were indeed loving me, but I was screening it out. I saw that unless others shared with me their love, I just would not be a good person.

Once I saw that I could not be a good person unless others shared with me their truth and their love, I realized others also needed my truth and my love in order to be good persons. I saw that although it was important to follow God's law, I could not be a good person unless I got close to others. That is why this second conversion was like break-

227

ing out of the woods. I recognized that although the Law of God was important, what I really needed was to live in love. On the throne of my heart, I put LOVE.

After a while, the grass ended and I began to climb up over rocks. My companions went ahead of me. All of sudden, I slipped a bit, and became very afraid. I felt very alone. All my energy drained out of me. I froze, unable to go up or go down. This symbolizes the *sudden trial* that happens on the spiritual journey. Perhaps someone very dear to me died, or I lost my physical or mental health. Maybe I made a mistake, which caused people no longer to trust me, and I wondered if I could trust my own judgment. Maybe I thought my whole life had been a waste, that I had let God down, and had led others astray. I felt God had abandoned me because I deserved it. I wondered if I had had any faith at all. Perhaps I would be lost forever. All I had on the throne of my heart was a question mark (?).

Deep down within myself, however, I heard a still voice that said all is well, that this was just a passing matter. My companions up ahead encouraged me to try to take a step, and then another, and another. I keep blindly on, putting my foot in this crevice and the next,—until all of a sudden I pulled myself over a rock, and could stand up. The whole mountain was supporting me. I had reached the top!

As I looked out in all directions, I saw an amazing sight of goodness and beauty. It seemed like I could reach out and touch what was at a great distance. I found welling up within myself an impulse to join all creatures in praising God.

I did not stay on the mountaintop. I ran down the mountain to tell others the good news that all things are in

God's hands. All we have to do is to let God be God,—that on the throne of our hearts we place GOD.

I know now that God will come to my aid in all my needs. I sense a new patience about the future and the present. I see, too, that those I love are also in God's hands, that God will see that they are cared for even when I am not present. I feel free now to be led wherever God wishes me to go. I understand now how simple it is to abandon myself to God, to submit to God's will in utter trust.

The study of the enneagram system as spirituality is something like climbing a mountain to reach the point of putting GOD on the throne of my heart. To abandon myself to God, I must not bypass obedience to God's will in the commandments and laws of the Church, nor overlook communion with others. These engagements, however, do not comprise the whole of union with God. There is an experience I yet need of being rescued directly by the hand of God, such that I will always know that, no matter what happens, the infinite power of God will support me, and that, as St. Paul says, "there is nothing in all of creation that will ever be able to separate us from the love God has for us..."[4]

Abandonment to God is born of confidence, or what Jesus calls "faith." This birth of confident faith cannot occur without an experience of losing control and needing to be rescued. This rescue, however, may occur within myself. I can get in touch with the lead of the Spirit, which is a power of grace from the divine source, but nevertheless is part of my being. I may be surprised by a new power in my life, giving me freedom from what in the past shackled my spirit. In enneagram terms, it is the grace that

---

[4] Rm 8:39

liberates me from my compulsion, a compulsion in which I once took pride, but now see for what it really was, *an addiction to self-fantasy.* It was a self-concept directed to a false sense of reality, as though I could be fulfilled without others, even without God.

C.
Enneagram Glossary

Enneagram Glossary

(* = cross reference)

Abandonment to God: a direct personal relationship with God characterized by an attitude of complete submission to God's will in utter trust. As an *intellectual conversion, abandonment to God is a way of seeing oneself as part and participant in all reality according to the plan of God.

Abiding peace: the *consolation which is experienced as a bold strengthening of faith, hope, and love along with a certitude that it is right for me to be in this present place doing this present action. Abiding peace is typical of the *head center, and is the predominant *consolation of *redeemed *Ones, *Threes, and *Sevens.

Acting against the compulsion: Moving against the *arrow of compulsion toward the *pride of the opposite *personality type. This effort is needed in order to be liberated from the blind power of the *compulsion.

Affective conversion: the healing or rectifying of the ruling *passion by its corresponding *virtue. Affective conversion follows from *intellectual conversion because the *heart center responds with *passionate love for the good of *fulfillment as seen by the *head center. By placing self-fulfillment in God's hands through *holy abandonment, the self is freed from the distortion of *passionate love caused by the attitude of *self-salvation.

Aggressive types: *personality types (1,3,8) whose preferred mode of behavior is to move against people as a *defensive strategy to protect the self and one's worth as a person. Each of these types has a different way of moving against others because each starts from a different *self-concept. Aggressive types act against their *compulsion by moving toward the mode of behavior typical of *compliant types: instead of being on the offensive against social reality, they become more accepting of the world as it is.

Anger: an attitude of being dissatisfied because things are not they way one wants them to be. Anger is the *passion characteristic of *Ones, who, as perfectionist personalities, resent what is imperfect.

Ant: the *totem of *redeemed *Ones who are well-organized and readily cooperate with others in tasks.

Appearances: the false or biased sense of reality characteristic of *compulsed *Threes. Their public image makes them feel good about themselves as successful when they are esteemed because of their accomplishments.

Apprehension: the false or biased sense of reality characteristic of *compulsed *Sixes, who feel they are in contact with real life only when they have fears about fulfilling what is expected of them.

Approval: the false or biased sense of reality characteristic of *compulsed *Twos, who do not feel good about themselves unless they are appreciated by another for the help they have given.

Arrogance: an aggressive attitude which seeks to intimidate others. Arrogance is the *passion characteristic of *Eights. By arrogance Eights protect themselves and attain a sense of *fulfillment by experiencing themselves as strong persons.

Arrow of compulsion: a pointer of the intersecting inner lines of the *enneagram, indicating the direction toward greater *compulsion. *Moving against the arrow decreases the force of one's *compulsion and moves one toward greater wholeness.

Authenticity: the *trap, or false idea, typical of *Fours, that by their own efforts they can attain *fulfillment by the perfect symbolic self-expression of all their deepest emotions. Because such authenticity is never attained, Fours who are trapped by authenticity always feel not quite themselves, as though they are waiting for their real life to begin.

Avoidance: that which expresses the basic *compulsion in each of the nine *personality types. People tend to take pride in the avoidance typical of their personality because they think this avoidance makes them superior to others.

Bald Eagle: the *totem of *redeemed *Threes who through conversion have abandoned themselves to God's Rule, such that they are at ease in being who they are without competing with others.

Basset hound: the *totem of *compulsed *Fours, who sit in their sadness as a way to become connected to others.

Being on fire: the *consolation originating in the total gift of self to God in love, whereby everything else is seen and loved in the context of God. Being on fire is typical of the *gut center and is the predominant consolation of *redeemed *Fours, *Fives, and *Sixes.

Being thankful: the *consolation which originates in seeing oneself separate from God yet very much loved by God. Being thankful is typical of the *heart center and is the predominant consolation of *redeemed *Twos, *Eights, and *Nines.

Black Stallion: the *totem of *redeemed *Fours who have come to understand that how they feel fits the present situation, with the result that they manifest a graceful self-possession.

Butterfly: the *totem of *redeemed *Sevens who know the beauty and joy they radiate comes out of a painful process they have experienced in the journey of their life.

Cat: the *totem of the *compulsed *Two, who though affectionate is very independent.

Centers: three fundamental ways in which human beings function with the use of conscious and dynamic energy, viz., the *gut center, the *heart center, and the *head center.

Co-creation: the *holy idea that abandonment to God involves one in working with God in God's creative work in history. This includes doing the work according to God's Plan, which, in particular involves one in the *paschal mystery. Co-creation is the *holy idea specific to *Sevens, with a particular emphasis on accepting the Cross in order to build up the Kingdom of God. As applied to *Sevens, the *holy idea of co-creation is needed for conversion from the *trap of *idealism.

Compassion: the *holy idea that God rules the world by forgiveness, tolerance, non-violence, and doing good to enemies. Compassion is the holy idea needed by *Eights for *conversion from the *trap of *justice so that they are set free from their penchant of lording over others.

Compliant types: *personality types (2,6,7) whose preferred mode of behavior is to move toward people. Each of these types has a different way of being dependent because each starts from a different *self-concept. Compliant types act against their *compulsion by moving toward the mode of behavior typical of *detached types. Instead of conforming to social reality they become more defensive.

Compulsed: the state of a *personality type under the domination of its *compulsion. A first step in becoming *redeemed is to discover and acknowledge one's hidden compulsion and *defensive strategy.

Compulsion: a basic driving force, typically hidden and unrecognized, which is channeled into a prevailing way of personal behavior. As long as the compulsion remains un-noticed, people will fail to understand themselves in their real motives. Each compulsion forms one of nine basic *personality types. The orientation of each compulsion is selfish, and expresses a form of *self-salvation, a basic way chosen to cope with life as under one's own control. It is a consequence of the *ego consciousness saying to the world, "I do not need you to be fully a person." Every compulsion is chosen as a way of life. Its hidden power is a specific strategy of avoiding something.

Consolation: a sense of well-being and inner joy occa-sioned by our being led by the Spirit in our orientation. The three basic consolations are (1) *being on fire, (2) *being grateful, and (3) *abiding peace.

Control: the false or biased sense of reality characteristic of *compulsed *Eights, such that they feel good about them-selves only when retaining power over others.

Conversion: the acceptance of salvation as coming from God rather than from oneself. Conversion is a radical ven-ture of entrusting oneself to God and his gracious guidance. There occurs a reliance on God's power and love in one's life. This reliance on God as the ground of one's being and the ground of all being results also in a trust in the well of one's energies even when one has lost control or made some mistake which could cause disaster to oneself.

Correctness: the false or biased sense of reality character-istic of *compulsed *Fives, who see fullness of life only in having overall insight without error or bias.

Courage: the *virtue characteristic of *redeemed *Sixes, which heals their *passion of *fear because they find their security in their divine adoption. Knowing that nothing can ever separate them from divine love (Rm 8:35-39), they find in themselves courage to do new things on their own and to make decisions when matters are tentative and risky.

Cowardice: a lack of resolution. Cowardice is the *ego-fixation of *Sixes because they tend to be afraid to act on the basis of their own free decisions because of self-doubt and anxiety.

Darkness: a *desolation similar to *turmoil, wherein the self feels weighed down and unable to respond. Darkness is a desolation of the *gut center, and is experienced espe-cially by *Twos and *Sevens.

Deceit: an attitude of seeking to persuade others to believe what is not true. Deceit is the *passion characteristic of *Threes. They use it to bring about their own success in the world through the manipulation of what others believe about them. Threes put their own feelings in a sack for the sake of presenting a good image before others. They be-come victims of their own deceit by identifying themselves with the image they have created so that they think they are good persons precisely because they are successful.

Deer: the *totem of *redeemed *Sixes who have learned to live in a relaxed way by discovering that God protects them and is always with them.

Defensive strategy: the way chosen by the *ego conscious-ness to compensate for the perceived loss of unity between the self and external reality by creating one's own life without being interdependent with external reality for personal *fulfillment. Defensive strategy always seeks to protect the self and one's worth as a person in confrontation with an alien world.

Desolation: the absence of a sense of well-being. The three areas of desolation include (1) *turmoil and *darkness, (2) *restlessness and *distaste, and (3) *rebelliousness, *despair, and *selfishness.

Despair: a *desolation wherein we feel ourselves to be without any value and thus without hope. Despair is a *desolation of the *head center and is experienced especially by *Nines.

Detached types: *personality types (4,5,9) whose preferred mode of behavior is to move away from people to enhance their own personal worth. Each of these types expresses this *defensive strategy in a different way because each starts with a different *self-concept. Detached types act against their *compulsion by moving toward the mode of behavior typical of *aggressive types. Instead of being defensive they become more offensive, or assertive, toward social reality.

Detachment: the *virtue characteristic of *redeemed *Fives, which heals their *passion of *stinginess, such that, instead of storing up resources for future eventualities, they live off the gifts of life day by day.

Diligence: the *virtue characteristic of *redeemed *Nines, which heals their *passion of *laziness. Having discovered God's unconditional love, Nines come to see the great worth of their unique selves, and consequently they take steps to learn skills and acquire credentials in order to be more of

service to others. The diligence of redeemed Nines is typically of that of laboring hour by hour and day by day.

Distaste: a *desolation experienced as a lack of faith, hope
and love or a lack of motivation to keep trying to pray or to
do good. Distaste is a desolation of the *heart center, and is
experienced especially by *Ones and *Fours.

Divine Providence: the *holy idea that God acts in our
lives to take care of all our real needs. Divine providence is
the holy idea needed by *Fives for *conversion from their
*trap of *knowledge. By acknowledging that whatever they
need to know will be provided by God through what happens in their lives, Fives become more willing to get involved with life, rather than just watch and reflect on it.

Efficiency: the *trap, or false idea, of *Threes which
evaluates the goodness of a person in terms of the ability to
achieve something. This makes life consist mainly in
achievements in competition with others. Because of this
trap, Threes believe that to be is to be successful. Consequently they consider failure as that which must be avoided
above all else in life.

Ego-consciousness: personal awareness as developed from
the split between the self and the world. The ego forms
itself by a *defensive strategy to protect the self from a
world perceived as alien. It limits the possible *fulfillment
of human *essence to a self-realization achievable by one's
own efforts, without the need of interdependence with external reality. Through ego-consciousness the person's fundamental love energies are distorted into *passions.

Ego-fixation: getting caught in a pattern of behavior that is
compulsive. Ego-fixation consists in failure to choose
something other than one's *compulsion as a way of life,
and represents a strategy set up by the *ego-consciousness

for *self-salvation. The ego-fixations of the nine *personality types are (1) *resentment, (2) *flattery, (3) *vainglory, (4) *melancholy, (5) *stinginess, (6) *cowardice, (7) *planning, (8) *vengeance, and (9) *indolence.

Eight: a *personality type characterized by the *avoidance of weakness. Eights glory in being strong persons. They are watchful lest others take advantage of them.

Elephant: the *totem of *compulsed *Nines who are ponderous and yet unaware of how much influence they have.

Enneagram: a term invented by George Ivanovich *Gurdjieff, to designate a nine-pointed figure which is both symbol and résumé of a system of *nine personality types said to be passed down in an oral tradition of the *sufis.

Envy: resentment toward those whose striking personality is seen as lessening one's own worth. Envy is the *passion characteristic of *Fours, who see themselves as superior to others in the way they express their unique feelings and refined style.

Equanimity: the *virtue characteristic of *redeemed *Fours, whereby their *passion of *envy is healed, such that they live their emotional lives with self-composure even when under stress.

Essence: all that a being is actually and potentially. In the *fall from society the *ego consciousness takes on a strategy for *fulfillment which limits one's essence to some one *personality type, where this specific personality is assumed to be the ideal way of being human.

Fall from society: the experience of alienation from the world when the child experiences its social environment as contradicting the deepest feelings and desires of the self. This occasions the development of an *ego-consciousness involving a *defensive strategy, which evolves into one of the nine *personality types as the chosen way to achieve self-fulfilment.

Fear: an attitude of insecurity because of perceived threats to one's well-being. Fear is the *passion specific to *Sixes. Because for *Sixes to be is to be responsible, they become apprehensive as to which way is right. They typically seek to overcome such uncertainty by loyalty to a rule or authority figure of their group.

Five: a *personality type characterized by the avoidance of emptiness. Fives are preoccupied with growing in their store of knowledge. It is important to them not to get involved in anything not helpful for learning something.

Flattery: acting in such a way as to gratify and please others so as to win approval from them. Flattery is the *ego-fixation of *Twos because of their mistaken idea that they can win love. They present themselves to a special other in ways designed to make themselves liked by that person, especially by serving some need they see in that person.

Four: a *personality type characterized by the avoidance of ordinariness. It is very important to Fours to be special. They are inclined to think others do not understand them because of the uniqueness of the feelings they have experienced, especially the sorrow and tragedy of the past.

Fox: the *totem of the *compulsed *Five who watches everything from a safe distance.

Fulfillment: The essential completeness of the person. True fulfillment involves the union of persons with exterior reality, which includes the whole cosmos and God within it. The longing for fulfillment springs from one's *essence, and, for that reason, fulfillment is the realization of one's deepest desire.

God's Will: The *holy idea of living in service of God's goals, objectives, and action plans. God's will is the holy idea needed by *Threes for *conversion from the *trap of *efficiency, so that they place God's administration of them and the world above their own administration.

Grace: the *holy idea that God's love is a free gift and cannot be won. Grace is the holy idea needed by the *Two to correct the false idea of *service which sees love as only a response of appreciation, and thus as something that can be gained by serving another's needs.

Growth: the*holy idea that the real perfection of creatures involves their being in the process of becoming, and that this is an expression of God governing the world in an evolutionary way. By the idea of growth, holiness is seen as a process of maturation rather than appropriating some norm of being complete and correct. Growth is the holy idea needed by the *One for *conversion from the *trap of *perfection.

Gurdjieff, George Ivanovich: Russian philosopher who is credited with introducing the enneagram to the West. He claimed to have learned it from the Sarmouni Brotherhood. His teachings are available in the work of one of his pupils, P.D. Ouspensky, *In Search of the Miraculous: Fragments of an Unknown Teaching* (Harcourt, Brace & World, 1949).

Gut center: the instinctive function through which conscious and dynamic energy reacts spontaneously. This gut center is concerned with being; it is typically experienced in habits.

Gut persons: *personality types (8,9,1) who have chosen their instinctive center as their preferred way of functioning. They typically enter a situation and say, "Here I am; deal with me." They seek control by the power of just being there.

Harmony: the false or biased sense of reality characteristic of *compulsed *Nines, who think that to have real life they must be at peace. To achieve that harmony, they often back off from conflict rather than deal with it.

Head center: the thinking function through which conscious and dynamic energy is experienced as deliberation. This head center is concerned with stepping back from reality as perceived and to reconstruct it according to some pattern of meaning.

Head persons: *personality types (5,6,7) who have chosen their thinking center as their preferred way of functioning. They typically enter a situation and ask, "How does this all fit together?" They seek control by knowing where everything fits.

Heart center: the feeling function through which conscious and dynamic energy is experienced in personal relationships. The heart center is concerned with emotions.

Heart persons: *personality types (2,3,4) who have chosen their feeling center as their preferred way of functioning. They typically enter a situation and ask, "Are you going to like me or not?" They seek control by providing something that will get a favorable response from another.

Holy abandonment: a direct personal relationship with God characterized by an attitude of complete submission to God's will in utter trust. As an *intellectual conversion, holy abandonment is a way of seeing oneself as part and participant in all reality according to the plan of God.

Holy idea: A truth about God which is a liberation from the *trap, or false idea, of how to live one's life for personal *fulfillment. Accepting the holy idea moves the self to rely on God in a specific way, thereby freeing the self from the *defensive strategy of its *compulsion. The holy ideas belonging to the nine types are (1) *Growth, (2)*Grace, (3) *God's Will, (4) *Union with God, (5) *Divine Providence, (6) *Trust in God, (7) *Co-creation, (8) *Compassion, and (9) *Unconditional Love.

Humility: the *virtue characteristic of *redeemed *Twos, whereby they are healed of their *passion of *pride, such that, by recognizing their own limitations and needs, they accept being helped by others.

Idealism: the *trap, or false idea, typical of *Sevens, stating that *fulfillment is obtained only through an environment of good cheer. Because of this trap of *idealism, *compulsed Sevens avoid and deny whatever is painful.

Indolence: an disinclination to focussed activity, such that one is distracted from doing one's job by small comforts of life. Indolence is the *ego-fixation of *Nines because of their poor sense of priorities and their lack of self-esteem.

Instinctual conversion: the awakening of the fruits of the Spirit in the *gut center, whereby we spontaneously respond to people and situations rather than react to them with a *defensive strategy. By instinctual conversion we are able to live in God's hands by moving with the instinct given by God's indwelling Spirit. This instinct gives us a connaturality to the good, the right, and the fulfilling. Thereby we experience *consolation when we are doing God's will and *desolation when we are not in accordance with the lead of the Spirit.

Intellectual conversion: the movement from the *trap to the *holy idea. Acceptance of the holy idea is basic to abandonment to God, whereby one moves out of a stance of *self-salvation and is opened to accepting a need for God to arrive at personal *fulfillment. Intellectual conversion is an opening to ultimate truth, and as such is crucial to being set free from *ego-fixation. This seeing and acceptance of ultimate truth is necessary before one can arrive at *affective conversion and true *instinctual conversion.

Irish setter: the *totem of *redeemed *Twos who are emotionally effusive and always ready to follow a friend.

Justice: the *trap, or false idea, typical of *Eights, that *fulfillment is attained ultimately by confrontation with whatever one sees as wrong with the world. Because of this trap of justice *compulsed Eights think that to be is to be strong, and have a disdain for any weakness in themselves or others.

Knowledge: the *trap, or false idea, of *Fives, stating that their *fulfillment consists in forming a correct judgment about everything solely through their own efforts. As a result Fives become great observers rather than participants in life, since they feel compelled to find all resources within themselves.

Laziness: the attitude of taking things easy. Laziness, or indolence, is the *passion characteristic of *Nines, whereby they seek to back away from tension, conflict, and strong feelings in order to be peaceful and content.

Melancholy: a mood of sweet regret for what has been lost. Melancholy is the *ego-fixation of *Fours, who dwell excessively on past tragedies in their lives.

Modes of behavior: ways of relating to the world. The fundamental modes of behavior in enneagram theory are aggressive (1,3,8), compliant (2,6,7), and detached (4,5,9).

Monkey: the *totem of *compulsed *Sevens who seems "up in the air" because of having so many things going on in their lives, and always ready to add more.

Moving against the arrow: the effort made to live with greater balance by taking on the *pride of the *personality type which stands opposite to the pointer of the *arrow of compulsion. This pride needs to replace the pride of one's own personality type in order to be opened up to an *instinctual conversion. *Aggressive types (1,3,8) become more accepting and receiving instead of being on the offensive against others. *Compliant types (2,6,7) become more detached instead of depending on others for fulfillment. *Detached types (4,5,9) stretch their personality by aggressive behavior instead of withdrawing to find fulfillment.

Moving with the arrow: giving way to greater compulsion by also taking on the *compulsion of the opposite type pointed to by the *arrows of compulsion. One is inclined to do this when under stress. *Aggressive types (1,3,8) fall into *despair by relinquishing their characteristic aggressive behavior and moving into withdrawing behavior. *Compliant types (2,6,7) fall into *presumption when they relinguish seeking *fulfillment by adaption to the world as it is and become aggressive. *Detached types (4,5,9) lose self-confidence and become dependent on some false or unrealistic hope.

Nine: a *personality type characterized by the *avoidance of conflict. Nines feel uncomfortable with any tension or lack of harmony between people. To *Nines nothing is as important as peace and restraint.

One: a *personality type characterized by the *avoidance of *anger. Ones are dedicated to being perfect and to doing things in a perfect way. Their *pride consists in being hard-working.

Over-indulgence: the attitude seeking an excess of pleasures. Over-indulgence (gluttony, intemperance) is the *passion characteristic of *Sevens, who tend to make pleasure an absolute good. Since pleasures are by their very nature limited, seeking unlimited pleasure engages the Seven into planning more enjoyments for the future.

Owl: the *totem of *redeemed *Fives who can be at rest while remaining alert, knowing that divine providence has prepared them for any involvement.

Paschal Mystery: the aspect of the divine economy according to which God brings new life through suffering and death. Acceptance of the paschal mystery is needed by *Sevens for *conversion from the *trap of idealism so that they accept the carrying of the cross as the necessary price to be paid for achieving any lasting good.

Passion: a dominant disposition wherein the self's responsive energy of love is distorted by a false sense of reality. This false sense of reality entails the mistake of seeing a limited good as though it were the absolute good of *fulfillment for the person. The specific passion of each of the nine *personality types are (1) *anger, (2) *pride, (3) *deceit, (4) *envy, (5) *stinginess, (6) *fear, (7) *over-indulgence, (8) *arrogance, (9) *laziness.

Passionate love: the human being's fundamental energy which pursues personal *fulfillment. The self will have a passionate love for whatever is viewed as its absolute good. Where that goal is less than the fullness of human *essence, passionate love causes the self to be unbalanced through the development of a *passion characteristic of its *personality type.

Peacock: the *totem of the *compulsed *Three, who seeks to get the attention of others out of vanity.

Perfection: the *trap, or false idea, typical of *Ones, stating that reality should not be incomplete or have anything out of order, such that "there is a place for everything and everything should be in its place." Because of this false idea, Ones become angry when they perceive themselves or the world as not perfect. They deny this *anger within themselves because their *trap of perfecction does not allow them to be content with having the imperfection of anger.

Personality type: a particular way of being a person which emerges out of choosing one of nine kinds of *ego-consciousness.

Planning: the false or biased sense of reality characteristic of *compulsed *Sevens, such that real life consists in their mental formulations of future happenings. Such mental formulations of future happenings are the *ego-fixation of *Sevens because by such planning they can maintain a high level of excitement and create multiple options rather than become committed to a single course of action.

Porpoise: the *totem of *redeemed *Nines who have found their life by belonging to a group and by being peacemakers wherever they are.

Presumption: a confidence in oneself or others which is false because it is not based on reality.

Pride: a) As the *passion characteristic of *Twos, pride is an attitude of not needing others. Through pride Twos deny they have any need in themselves. This is their *defensive strategy to keep control by having others need them. b) As the specific attitude of each *personality type, pride is the attitude of what is most important in being a person, and that which makes one superior to others. Instead of trying to live out the whole spectrum of possibilities as a person, compulsive persons see the pride specific to their personality type as making them superior to others.

Rabbit: the *totem of the *compulsed *Six who lives with much *apprehension and indecision.

Redeemed: the state of a *personality type no longer under the domination of its characteristic *compulsion. This liberation from the compulsion's domination is called *redemption.

Redemption: the act or process of paying a price to release captives from slavery. As applied to the *enneagram, redemption is the paying of a price to overcome one's *compulsion through three sources of help: oneself, others, and God. This is seen as "paying a price" because overcoming a compulsion involves actions contrary to one's inclinations.

Resentment: a feeling of indignant displeasure because someone or something is not the way it should be. Resentment is the *ego-fixation of *Ones because of the great importance they give to *perfection.

Restlessness: a *desolation experienced as inner agitation which expresses itself in frenzied activity. Restlessness is a desolation of the *heart center, and is experienced especially by *Sixes.

Rhinoceros: the *totem of *compulsed *Eights who instinctively defend themselves by aggression..

Scripts: the false or biased sense of reality characteristic of *compulsed *Fours, who withdraw to rehearse how to express themselves, since they see their fulfillment only in the authentic expression of their unique feelings.

Security: the *trap, or false idea, typical of *Sixes, stating that salvation from self-doubt and indecision comes through obedience to authorities and laws. Because of this trap of security, compulsed Sixes see deviance as the greatest evil. As a consequence, they view life as full of demands to which they are obliged to respond to be acceptable as persons.

Self-abasement: the *trap, or false idea, typical of *Nines, that there is not much of worth within themselves and that their energy has to come from some outside source. Because of self-abasement, *compulsed Nines have little sense of priorities and consider that whatever they do is of little value.

Self-concept: a way of looking at the self. The fundamental self-concepts in enneagram theory are "I am bigger than the world" (the independent 2,5,8), "I must adjust to the world" (the self-absorbed 3,6,9), and "I am smaller than the world" (the stubborn 1,4,7).

Self-salvation: the attitude that one's essential completeness as a person, or one's *fulfillment, can be attained solely by oneself. The attitude of self-salvation springs from the *fall from society, where persons experience such a contradiction between themselves and society that they no longer believe they can realize their deepest desires through union with exterior reality. This involves a necessary limiting in the awareness of what fulfillment is.

Selfishness: a *desolation wherein we don't feel like responding to the good we see ourselves receiving from others. Selfishness is a desolation of the *head center, and is experienced especially by *Fives who withdraw from others who love them, and by *Eights who give up being strong persons.

Serenity: the *virtue characteristic of *redeemed *Ones, whereby their *passion of *anger is healed such that they live with consistent self-composure.

Service: the *trap, or false idea, characteristic of *Twos, stating that to be they must be of help to the need of another. By the idea of service, *Twos deny that they themselves have any need and they falsely think of themselves as totally selfless.

Seven: a *personality type characterized by the avoidance of pain. Sevens think life should not be experienced as painful in any way. Often they fail to carry out what they have planned because of the discomfort entailed in execution.

Shoulds: the false or biased sense of reality characteristic of *compulsed *Ones, who see real life coming only if things are made better. They feel good about themselves only by correcting what is wrong and doing what is right externally. Consequently, they are great criticizers, both of themselves and others.

Simplicity: the *virtue characteristic of *redeemed *Eights, which heals their *passion of *arrogance. Having placed all judgment in God's hands, as taught by Jesus in

Mt 7:1ff, *Eights become able to take things at face value without probing and testing people. Simplicity leads *Eights to be non-violent in the way they seek to establish justice.

Six: a *personality type characterized by the *avoidance of deviance. Sixes see life as filled with demands, and they strive to avoid any neglect of duty. They see this as being loyal to the group to which they belong.

Sobriety: the *virtue characteristic of *redeemed *Sevens, whereby their *passion of *over-indulgence is healed by a practical acceptance of the *paschal mystery in their lives. By this they become earnest in bearing whatever pain is needed to give birth to some of their dreams and ideals.

Stinginess: an attitude of clinging to what is one's own rather than sharing it or giving it to others. Stinginess is the *ego-fixation of *Fives and also their *passion. By being stingy with their possessions and by avoiding commitments, *Fives seek independence from others and private space in order to work on their own projects. Because they experience emptiness in themselves they see their security and worth as consisting in holding on to what they have and building it up irrespective of whether or not it can be of benefit to others.

Sufis: members of a movement of Muslim mysticism which is credited with transmitting the original oral tradition of the *enneagram.

Terrier: the *totem of *compulsed *Ones, who are always worrying about what is going on around them and overestimate themselves in setting things right. Like terriers, they "snap at the heels" of others as they point out what is wrong.

Three: a *personality type characterized by the *avoidance of failure. Threes identify themselves with being successful in the eyes of others.

Tiger: the *totem of *redeemed *Eights who have power but because they are sensitive to people they can wait for the right moment to use that power for the good of others.

Totems: animals which symbolize the nine *personality types. Those of the *compulsed personality types are *terrier (1), *cat (2), *peacock (3),*basset hound (4),*fox (5),*rabbit (6),*monkey (7),*rhinoceros (8), and *elephant (9). Those of the *redeemed personality types are *ant (1),*Irish setter (2),*bald eagle (3), *black stallion (4), *owl (5), *deer (6), *butterfly (7), *tiger (8), and *porpoise (9).

Trap: a habitual way of acting derived from *ego consciousness. The trap involves getting caught in a pattern of behavior that is compulsive.

Trust in God: the *holy idea that the basis of our ultimate security is God's parental love for us as his adopted children. This is the *holy idea needed by *Sixes for *conversion from the false idea that ultimate security is obtained through the keeping of laws and norms.

Truthfulness: the virtue characteristic of *redeemed Threes, whereby their *passion of *deceit is healed by personal disclosure.

Turmoil: the *desolation experienced as inner confusion. Turmoil is a desolation of the *gut center, and is experienced especially by *Threes when they feel driven to keep moving in circles without getting anywhere.

Two: a *personality type characterized by the *avoidance of need. Twos are preoccupied with noticing the needs of others. Their *pride is in being helpful, especially to a special someone.

Unbalanced self: the living out of human *essence with a lack of wholeness or integration. Since human essence is realized in nine ways of personality, the limiting of one's fulfillment to anything less than all these nine ways constitutes such an unbalanced self. Wholeness can be restored to the unbalanced self by *intellectual conversion, *affective conversion, and *instinctive conversion.

Unconditional Love: the *holy idea that we are lovable simply because of who we are. This idea of unconditional love is needed by *Nines for *conversion from the *trap of *self-abasement.

Union with God: the *holy idea that the way to personal *fulfillment is by a journey to God. This means a reliance on God's action to make use of all of one's life experiences for developing the unique creative idea God has for each person as a special gift to the world at this time in history. Union with God is the *holy idea needed by *Fours for *conversion from the false idea of attaining their *authenticity by their own efforts, which are often theatrical.

Vainglory: the presentation of an image of oneself that is designed to gain esteem from others. Vainglory is the *ego-fixation of *Threes because they consider that their worth as persons consists in being successful in the eyes of others.

Value: that which is of unlimited worth, such that it calls upon persons for a commitment entailing personal sacrifice. Values remain merely ideas until they are incarnated by personal commitment. Examples of gospel values are mercy, justice, and fidelity. *Sixes in particular need to take on a morality of values in order to become healthy and balanced.

Vengeance: retaliation for the sake of balancing the scales of justice. Vengeance is the *ego-fixation of *Eights, who believe that to be strong is to be good, and thus wish to bring suffering to anyone who humiliates or contradicts them.

Virtue: a permanent disposition which moves a person toward a full life and true fulfillment. Each virtue heals a specific *passion, which is a distortion of *passionate love. The virtues specific to each *enneagram types are (1) *serenity, (2) *humility, (3) *truthfulness, (4) *equanimity, (5) *detachment, (6) *courage, (7) *sobriety, (8) *simplicity, and (9) *diligence.

Wings: the *personality type adjacent on each side of a given number on the *enneagram. It is commonly thought that a given personality type often leans toward one of its wings, taking on some of the characteristics of that personality type also. Wings may also be considered as resting in the *center adjacent to an enneagram point. According to this latter theory the three denial points (3,6,9) do not have wings, because their adjacent enneagram point has chosen the same preferred center, and each of the other points has only one wing, since the point on the other side has the same preferred center. From this it follows that besides functioning well in one's own preferred center, one also performs well in one's wing.